NICHOLAS CARDINAL WISEMAN

Nicholas Cardinal Wiseman

A VICTORIAN PRELATE
AND HIS WRITINGS

S. W. Jackman

THE FIVE LAMPS PRESS

Set in Times Roman type
and printed by The Dolmen Press Limited,
North Richmond Industrial Estate, North Richmond Street,
Dublin 1, Ireland,
for The Five Lamps Press

European Distributor :
Colin Smythe Ltd., Gerrards Cross, Bucks., U.K.

Canadian Distributor :
Sono Nis Press, 1745 Blanshard St., Victoria, B.C., Canada

American Distributor :
The University Press of Virginia,
Box 3608, University Station, Charlottesville, Virginia 22903, U.S.A.

ISBN 0-901072-70-2

In piam memoriam

Erskine Childers
(1905-1973)

Acknowledgements

This volume does not pretend to be a definitive study of Nicholas Wiseman; rather it is intended to present the man and his works and to suggest where he belongs in the over-all milieu of nineteenth century studies. I wish here to acknowledge how much I owe to the late Col. the Rt. Rev. Monsignor Francis Cave who initially introduced me to the writings of Nicholas Wiseman. I am also obligated to Father Mark Tierney, O.S.B., who encouraged and promoted my interest in the subject. To the University of Victoria and the Canada Council I wish to express my thanks for grants-in-aid for research. As always the counsel and advice given to me by Walter Whitehill was much appreciated. My thanks also to the many others who made valuable suggestions or provided help and assistance when asked and thereby made publication of the manuscript possible. I am indebted to the Master and Fellows of St. Edmund's House in Cambridge for their friendship and hospitality. Mrs. Whitfield coped with the typing of the manuscript and I herewith wish to express my thanks. In particular I should like to take this occasion to say how grateful I am to Andrew Carpenter who read the manuscript, made many wise and useful suggestions for its improvement and who generously undertook to see the manuscript through the press.

Contents

1

A Portrait Sketch

Every age is one of contradiction, yet each generation thinks itself infinitely more rational than that which preceded it. To the twentieth century, which has seen the decline of religious orthodoxy and the diminution of church attendance, there seems nothing strange in applauding liberal thinkers who insist on the secularization of all public life, while at the same time admiring the Anglo-Catholicism of T. S. Eliot or accepting Jesus-freaks as perfectly natural phenomena. On the other hand, the contemporary world is highly censorious of what it calls the hypocritical Victorian morality and the excessive place of religion in all aspects of life, regarding it as psychologically unsound and intellectually and socially dishonest. Yet, the modern world has its own hypocrisies which may be just as damaging to the human personality as the apparent obscurantism of our forebears. We may not believe in religion, certainly not in the traditional sense; but the legions who follow the Indian mystics, who embark upon courses in meditation and Zen are seeking answers to problems which seem to transcend ordinary reason. To talk about Christianity in the orthodox meaning of the word is not *comme il faut* in fashionable intellectual circles; but to discuss with tedious earnestness — one almost adds Victorian piety — of the benefits of Yoga or some such is quite acceptable. It is merely an example that change is no change; only the nomenclature is different and the Master of Zen has replaced the Archbishop as being 'significant'.

A century ago the Christian church was still a vital force; to be sure, it was under attack by the rationalists but its essential order was secure. To emphasize this point, one should remember that the general public over much of the earth's surface assumed that mankind was or ought to be Christian, and took umbrage with those in their midst who tried to opt out of this designation. Countries were given denominational tags; France and Spain, for example, were Roman Catholic, while Britain, Germany and the United States were Protestant. Indeed, the national church seemed to indicate the foibles and weaknesses of character. To the average Englishman a papist country was untrustworthy and benighted, while a Protestant nation was reliable and progressive. The contrary view might well be held by those who were Roman Catholics.

By standards of the last century, England, Wales and Scotland were reckoned to be Protestant countries while Ireland was accepted as Roman Catholic. In England and Wales the Church of England was the established church, while in Scotland the Church of Scotland held the same position. Apart from these official churches there was a large body of Protestant dissenters who made up the membership of the nonconformist denominations. Even in Ireland the Protestants were important, if not numerically, at least socially and politically. For much of the nineteenth century, the Church of Ireland was an officially established religious body and part of the Anglican communion. It had power and privilege, and it was the church of 'the ascendancy' — the ruling class. The Presbyterians were not insignificant in Ireland either, for they had adherents throughout the country and particularly in the north.

Yet despite all this, relatively few Protestant clergymen of any denomination in England, Wales or Ireland made more than an ephemeral impression upon the permanent consciousness of society. Who now remembers Tait, Sumner or Benson, all leading Anglican ecclesiastics in their own day? Even the less exalted, such as Kingsley or Keble, are recollected only dimly. Moreover, the Church of Scotland does little better, even in a country where the hold of the church on the public mind of the educated classes was more secure, and where presumably its leaders would have made a greater impact upon the membership. But the nonconformist tradition is little better represented; only Booth of the Salvation Army possibly evokes a flicker of recognition in a few.

The Roman Catholic Church has done slightly better. Henry Edward Manning may well be remembered by a generation that read *Eminent Victorians* for the savageness of the portrait created by Strachey. John Henry Newman may very well do the best of all. Somehow this man has managed to remain a vital entity, perhaps because of the strangeness of his history, perhaps because of his timeless mystical writings, or perhaps because he meant so much to his own time that he transcended his age.

Newman owes much of his fame, not to Manning whose destiny it was to be tied inexorably to him for good or ill, but to another Roman Catholic cleric who is now not even remembered by most of his own church. This individual is Nicholas Wiseman. To be sure there is a Wiseman Society and a *Wiseman Review* but who knows anything about Wiseman himself? The student of literature may be dimly aware that he was the prototype for Browning's poem *Bishop Blougram's Apology* or that, coupled with Manning, he was used to create the composite cardinal in Disraeli's novel *Lothair*. The professional historian has met him as a protagonist

10

in the 'No popery' business of 1850 but as a living figure Wiseman has sunk almost without a trace. He has joined his Anglican, nonconformist and Presbyterian brethren in being placed in Clio's waste-bin; but in his own day and generation his impact both on his own co-religionists and upon society at large in Britain, Ireland and in Rome was not insignificant. There is little doubt that through his efforts the Anglican converts of the 1840's found a sympathy and understanding which otherwise might not have been theirs. Singlehanded he may have done much to transform the English Roman Catholic community from an introverted society with distinctly Gallican sympathies to one that was extroverted and ultramontanist.

If one wished to combine in one person three elements most likely to bring out all of the latent — or, indeed, not so latent — prejudices of the last century in Great Britain, it would be to say that an individual was Irish in origin, Spanish by birth and Roman Catholic by education and religion. All of these elements were possessed by Nicholas Wiseman. They were to help to provide him with sources of strength but at the same time they were to be the roots of many of his difficulties with his contemporaries. As if these three elements were not in themselves enough, Wiseman had a fourth which compounded them all: he was an ordained priest of the Roman Catholic Church and, almost universally, such clerics were regarded with the gravest suspicion by all but their co-religionists. Moreover, it was in his priestly, and later in his episcopal, office that he became a figure in national life, and to 'good' Protestants he behaved almost precisely as they imagined Roman Catholic clerics would do, thereby confirming all of their worst apprehensions and fears.

Nicholas Wiseman[1] was the second son of James and Xaviera Wiseman. The latter's family, the Stranges, were particularly pious and had named their daughter after the great St. Francis Xavier. The Wisemans resided in Seville and it was here that their son was born on 2 August 1802.[2] When the infant was baptized, his mother dedicated him to the service of the church; hence, almost from birth, his destiny seemed to be inextricably bound up with religious beliefs. When Nicholas Wiseman was three years old, his father died and his widow with her children — two sons and a daughter — retired to Ireland where they had family connections and numerous friends. The little boys were sent to a local school in Waterford but this institution was not entirely satisfactory for a number of reasons, some social and some academic, and they were withdrawn and sent to Ushaw College in England. At about the same time Xaviera Wiseman moved to Durham, making her home not too far from where her sons were being educated.

Young Nicholas Wiseman seems to have made little or no impact on the school; indeed, he always assumed, so later reports imply, that his school-fellows thought him somewhat dull. Initially he did not show signs of being a great scholar and thus was not marked out for special attention and approbation by his teachers, but in his last year at Ushaw he was at the head of his class. Moreover, he was not outstanding at games, and though this was well before such schools often became 'athletocracies', games were important to the boys themselves. In sum, at this stage he was just an ordinary boy, no more and no less.

As a school, Ushaw College had a reputation for strict discipline and extreme piety. Religious activities were emphasized and the school chapel services were the central theme of daily life. Attendance at Mass was compulsory — it would have been impossible for the staff to have conceived of any deviation from such a regulation — as were other daily services, while fast and holy days were observed strictly and without question. The general effect on the boys was to confirm and strengthen their religious convictions with the result that a number of them chose to enter the priesthood, and Wiseman's decision to do likewise is hardly surprising. One of his immediate contemporaries to follow the same path was George Errington. The careers of these two were to be bound together inextricably, and, in the end, with unhappy consequences for both.

His stay at Ushaw came to an end when he was sixteen. As one committed to a religious vocation, he was chosen to go to Rome where he was to become a student in the recently reopened English College. After the usual round of farewell visits to family and friends, he embarked on 2 October 1818. The long sea-voyage to Italy was not without incident: during the passage a man fell overboard and was drowned, the ship caught fire, and a dog and a passenger went mad. After such a journey it is perhaps not surprising that Wiseman and his fellow travellers were not at all sad when the vessel finally reached her destination. The close confinement and the inactive life were most tedious, and even the adventures did little to relieve the inevitable boredom.

Once ashore he was very impatient to reach Rome itself; when he finally saw the city, he was overwhelmed with its magnificence and grandeur. These feelings, combined with the religious associations of the place, brought from him all the ecstatic reactions that have been experienced by so many over the centuries.

The English College, which was to be his new home, had been disused for a number of years but, although it was shabby, the building was in reasonable repair. True, the old church next door was roofless, but the chapel attached to the college, if somewhat unkempt, was generally intact; the library was in disarray and the books in a chaotic state, but with a little work they could soon be restored to full use. But Wiseman was later to observe, despite everything 'one felt at once at home; . . . it was English ground, a part of the fatherland, a restored inheritance.'[3]

As a very spacial mark of esteem, Wiseman and five fellow collegians were received in audience by Pope Pius VII on Christmas Eve. The aged pontiff, who had survived so many vicissitudes and who in himself was the symbol of the Church restored from war and revolution, greeted his young guests in an affable and easy fashion. They were, however, somewhat overawed by their surroundings and by their host, and conversation did not proceed very easily. The Pope asked the usual questions and received the traditional responses. The audience was not prolonged, but before dismissing his guests Pius VII observed: 'I hope you will do honour to Rome and to your country.'[4] For Wiseman this particular papal admonition was to be one of the guiding precepts of his life; and while he was later to have many, and more intimate, contacts with the incumbents of the Chair of St. Peter, none was ever to affect him quite as this initial one had done.

For the next six years he was to live the life of a student. As at Ushaw, the regimen was austere, the studies exacting and the life generally far from easy. Yet Wiseman loved every minute of it. While his daily existence was somewhat circumscribed, the fact that he resided in Rome ensured that life was far from dull. The city of Rome is rarely boring and Wiseman never found his stay there tedious. Although not occupying a position of eminence as a mere student in the English College, he was an intrinsic part of the papal capital, participating in many aspects of Roman life and on great occasions he was at least a privileged spectator. He worked hard at his studies and made some good friends, many of whom were already prominent in ecclesiastical circles, or were to become so in due course; these acquaintances were often to have considerable influence on his later career.

It was not all work nor was it all being part of the great world. Wiseman and his fellow seminarians, like other people, went for holidays in the country during the summer; they visited galleries, attended concerts and entertained their friends in the college. Wiseman himself described existence in college: 'The life of the student in Rome should be one of unblended enjoyment. . . .'[5] Certainly, later, he was always to regard his days as a seminarian with a certain amount of romantic nostalgia. While he would probably have never admitted it public, his sojourn in the English

College were 'the happiest days of his life.'

This untrammelled and irresponsible existence could not continue for ever; examinations must be sat and passed, essays and theses written and approved. On 7 July 1824 he formally submitted his thesis for the degree of doctor of divinity. There was a public examination attended by friends and interested persons. Among those present was Father Capellari who later became Pope Gregory XVI and who was to be one of Wiseman's most important patrons, as well as a good friend. Wiseman performed well at the examination: his defence of his thesis was highly satisfactory and the examiners were pleased to award him his degree. A few days later — as a sort of climax to the whole affair and in the mediaeval student fashion — he then gave a dinner for the examiners and his friends. He could now call himself Doctor Wiseman.

Before beginning an active career in the Church, he permitted himself a holiday and went to France. He was very much the typical tourist in Paris and saw the principal sights and museums; but the theatres and the like which most visitors deemed an essential part of Parisian life were obviously omitted. He spent a good deal of time with his mother and sister who were then residing not far from the French capital. He was away from Rome for several months, only returning in the late autumn, and he travelled overland and visited a number of Italian cities in the process. His letters are full of his enthusiasm for all that he saw during his travels.

Almost immediately upon his return to Rome he received minor orders — the ceremony took place a week before Christmas — and some three months later, on 10 March 1825, he was ordained a priest. His career had now officially begun. The initial step in fulfilling his vocation was taken; what followed thereafter would depend partly upon his own abilities and partly upon the orders given to him by his superiors.

One of the first advantages of his new position as priest and doctor of divinity was that he was no longer subject to the collegiate discipline as a seminarian, but was now able to direct his existence as he chose. To be sure, he had the usual priestly obligations but as yet no definite duties beyond these. As a result, much of his time was passed in various libraries doing private scholarly research. However, he occasionally indulged himself in expeditions to the countryside but he did not allow these pleasures to make large incursions into his life. Academic concerns predominated.

His erudition and his general probity of manner gained him much approbation in ecclesiastical circles and, as a result, he was

14

named vice-rector of his college in 1827. He also applied for the professorship of oriental languages at the university, but the authorities had decided that in this instance the post would be filled by a scholar of international repute and not be open to general competition. Wiseman protested against such a procedure and appealed to the Pope himself. Before the latter could act, however, the university officials formally designated an incumbent for the chair. Wiseman was crestfallen; however, he refused to accept defeat and made a new application requesting that his own published works be compared with those of the official nominee. He based his claim chiefly upon his *Horae Syriacae* which had appeared only a short time previously and which had been highly praised by a number of scholars. After further consideration, the university authorities acknowledged that his was the superior work, withdrew their own nominee, and elected Wiseman the new professor of oriental languages. This incident is indicative of the man in many ways. He was very conscious of his rights and his abilities; he was always willing to be judged on his actions and merits but at the same time showed a grim determination, almost an obstinacy, in seeing things to the end. On this occasion his opponents apparently bore him no malice: but such was not always to be the case.

His success did not bring him immediate satisfaction because he was exhausted by the effort of his campaign and he had a minor breakdown. He began to suffer from acute insomnia, feared he was going mad, and, what was more terrifying to him, had doubts about his religious beliefs. Outwardly, he managed to remain calm enough, but inwardly all was in turmoil. In an attempt to alleviate his unhappiness, he undertook to establish an orderly regimen for himself; he continued to work hard but without the excessive pressures demanded of him while a candidate for his doctoral degree, and he spent much time in prayer and meditation. After some months of real mental anguish he slowly began to recover, and he gradually returned to a more relaxed and easy state of mind. He noted in his diary on his twenty-sixth birthday that he hoped 'the next and following years of my life may be spent more to the purpose for myself and others than my last and those which preceded it. Made good determinations — may they not prove like those which have vanished before them.' [6]

Following the departure of the rector of the English College in June 1828, Wiseman was named as temporary head; but he was the obvious person to assume the post on a permanent basis, and he was formally appointed six months later. By accepting this office, he had committed himself to a full-time career in Rome, for such was the accepted procedure. In his case things ultimately

15

were to be different, but at that time it would not have appeared to be so.

He took his duties extremely seriously; his scholarly abilities and academic reputation gave him all the authority that might be required over the staff and the students alike, but his real power came from his personal character. He was very easy and affable with everyone, and, hence, had no difficulties in getting the co-operation of all members of the English College. In addition to his administrative duties, he also acted as the channel of much information on matters relating to England. He tried to mediate in the controversy between Bishop Baines and the monks at Downside, and while he had only a limited success in this venture, he showed much tact on this occasion. His general reputation for discretion and for good sense gave him the credibility needed as a reliable reporter on all aspects of English life. Indeed, it should be emphasized that at no time did he ever think of himself as anything but English. His Irish background he seems to have almost completely forgotten; the only thing that might be considered Irish in origin was his emphasis on his religious faith.

As rector of the college he entertained many and varied guests: numerous British and American visitors came, as did Roman and European friends, for Wiseman genuinely liked people. He was gregarious and at the English College he had the means and facilities to entertain easily and well. His hospitality became proverbial: but it was not all for pleasure, because his many guests kept him well-informed and provided him with material which might well be useful to his ecclesiastical superiors. Certainly his rôle as host was one of his rectorial duties which gave him the most enjoyment.

Yet life was not as simple as it seemed. The political situation in the Roman states gave cause for concern, and although the government managed to keep things generally under control and the Carbonari under surveillance, many problems were still unresolved. Wiseman, essentially conservative and a loyal servant of the papacy, naturally favoured the *status quo*. To him it was only the foolish and sentimental intellectual liberals, combined with a few dangerous and subversive revolutionaries, who were actively involved in plotting against the authorities. However, Wiseman was not totally uncritical and he recognized that there were very real inequalities in the political and social system; at the same time he believed they were resolvable by means other than violence. His views on the situation in Rome were expressed most directly in letters to friends in the United States. To them he was, perhaps, more open and candid than to most other people. Indeed, as well as serving as a source of British news to his Roman superiors, he

16

was also an unofficial commentator on the latter to American colleagues who were always filled with curiosity about the Holy See but were not often well-informed about its activities.

He very soon exhausted himself by taking on too much responsibility, and his doctors required him to take more rest. He compromised, and while he resumed his scholarly life, he curtailed his participation in public affairs. At this time he received two guests who were portents for the future, John Henry Newman and Hurrell Froude. The three clerics had some lively and interesting conversations but the Anglicans were soon informed that, to Wiseman's way of thinking, reconciliation without submission was impossible. Despite their present differences, he had liked his guests and found them truly sympathetic.

As a result of his more restricted existence, Wiseman's general mental and physical state was much improved. He observed in March 1834: 'I feel as though the freshness of childhood's thoughts had once more returned to me, my heart expands with renewed delight. . . . I might almost say that I am leading a life of spiritual epicureanism, opening all my senses to a rich draught of religious sensations.' [7] This renewal of confidence and restoration of health was accompanied by new tasks. Wiseman believed that a Roman Catholic university should be founded — possibly in Ireland — but the place was not fixed. In this project he had the strong support of Bishop Baines, one of the Vicars Apostolic, but he also felt that the Roman Catholic community in Britain could be well served with a literary journal of merit. To bring these projects into reality it was decided that he would leave the English College for a time — officially he remained the rector — and go to England. Prior to leaving, he gave a series of public lectures — he had done so previously in 1827 and had gained much praise — and this time he chose to talk on science; the lectures were later published as *Lectures on the Connexion between Science and Revealed Religion.* The topic was a popular one, he had a good audience, and his command of the subject surprised many who were present. Once the lectures were completed he made the necessary preparations for his departure to England. From all indications it would appear that he knew somehow that this was a momentous journey and that he realized also that the old life in Rome was unlikely to be revived.

It was hard to leave and his preparations were leisurely; he did not finally depart from Rome until early summer, travelling overland. He stopped in Munich to see Döllinger, who at this time was a strong adherent of the papal position, and then he moved on to Paris to see other friends, finally reaching London on 14 July 1835.

He was put up by Bishop Bremerton in London and from this vantage-point he was able to make an initial survey of the Roman Catholic Church and its membership. The Church was no longer proscribed by law — emancipation having occurred in 1829 — but the community as a whole was still very cautious. The long years of persecution had filled it with distrust and it was still a very inward-looking society. Wiseman felt this attitude backward and thought that the need was for action.

He moved on to Prior Park, where Bishop Baines had established himself, but the sojourn here was not a very happy one; Bishop Baines patronized Monsignor Wiseman. Moreover, it was clear that while Baines was still enthusiastic about the university, he did not want Wiseman, who had too many ideas of his own, to be in charge. Moreover, Wiseman saw the university as a 'beginning of a new era for Catholic affairs, in education, in literature, in public position . . .',[8] but Baines wanted it for his own purposes, largely as a training college for the priesthood and to isolate the Roman Catholics from the snares of the Protestant world. Although the two were outwardly cordial, it was clear that their views were far from harmonious and that collaboration was impossible.

After this initial failure, he quite sensibly decided to take a better look at the situation in England and he went on a 'progress', staying with 'such of the nobility or gentry of these realms as can sufficiently appreciate such an honour.'[9] He was a bit snobbish, and made it clear that he did not intend to put up in local inns or hotels. He went to Birmingham where he found Bishop Walsh, the local Vicar Apostolic, more congenial than his colleagues in London or at Prior Park. Wiseman was also a guest of Lord Shrewsbury at Alton Towers. He enjoyed himself with the peer and in the splendid surroundings, describing them as 'princely towers and enchanted gardens'.[10]

At this juncture Bishop Walsh proposed that Wiseman, much to the latter's surprise, should become his successor and be appointed coadjutor, but for the moment nothing was done. His future was not yet secured in England. After completing his tour of the midlands and visiting friends, Wiseman went back to London. Upon his return he was invited to assume charge of the chapel of the Sardinian Embassy in London on a temporary basis. He accepted and began his duties in November. He stayed with the Bagshawes who found him a most engaging man — lively, amusing and good company.

As priest in charge of the Sardinian chapel he took the regular Sunday services, giving the sermon in Italian. His facility with languages was famous: he not only spoke the usual European languages, German, French and Italian, but was also knowledgeable in the more arcane ones, speaking fluent Persian and Arabic for example. At this time he also gave a series of lectures entitled *Lectures on the Principal Doctrines and Practices of the Catholic Church* which were most successful, and he was invited to give a similar series in the spring. Wiseman's lectures were well attended, often by Protestants as well as his co-religionists, for it was probably the first public occasion since the Reformation upon which Roman Catholic theology and doctrine were expounded for an intelligent audience in England. He avowed that he did not intend to indulge in theological controversy: 'I must own that I have a great dislike — almost, I will say, an antipathy — to the name; for it supposes that we consider ourselves as in a state of warfare with others; that we adopt the principle which I reprobated . . . of establishing the truth of our doctrines by overthrowing others.' [11]

Generally speaking, Wiseman's moderation and the sensible way in which he presented his ideas both verbally and later in print received considerable approbation. A few bigoted Anglican clerics were very displeased and said some harsh things. Oddly enough, some Roman Catholics were also dissatisfied with Wiseman's lectures, feeling that they were not critical enough of heretical doctrine. Newman, still a member of the Church of England, reviewed the printed lectures in an article in the *British Critic* in which he pointed out the value of Catholic doctrines for his fellow Anglicans. The consequences of this were that some of the latter took more offence with Newman and his ideas than they did with Wiseman himself.

The general success of the lectures so delighted the mass of the Roman Catholic community in London that they presented Wiseman with a gold medal; on the obverse was his own likeness, on the reverse various religious symbols such as the papal tiara, the keys and a cross. While the medal was an agreeable souvenir, a more significant reaction to his lectures came in the invitation to write for the *Penny Cyclopedia* on the Roman Catholic Church; this would ensure that his views had an even wider audience. At the same time he also became involved in a controversy with John Poynder who had attacked the Roman Catholic Church; Wiseman replied in a series of letters, all of which were printed, and it was evident that his defence was more able than Poynder's attack. Even as staunch a Protestant as Gladstone was impressed, for he observed that Wiseman's statements, 'struck me as masterpieces of clear and unanswerable argument.' [12]

If the plan to establish a Roman Catholic university were shelved,

19

the second project, the establishment of a literary journal, was more easy to accomplish. The new publication was called the *Dublin Review* and the first issue appeared in May 1836. As for its editorial policy, he was to stipulate 'that no extreme political views should be introduced into the Review, . . .',[13] As well as serving as editor, he was to write many articles during the long years with which he was to be associated with it. A century and a quarter after its foundation, the journal changed its name to *The Wiseman Review* to honour the man who had created it and who had determined its intellectual direction and high literary standard.

With the *Dublin Review* formally launched, it was now time for him to return to Rome. He waited until the second number of the journal was published and began the journey in early September 1836. He went from London to Paris, where he made a short halt and by the end of the month was once more in Rome.

He soon reassumed his position as rector of the English College and occupied his time completely with his duties; but his heart was not in it, and he personally wished to return to England. Nevertheless, he started to lecture once more at the university, and at the same time busied himself with the general welfare of his collegians. He accompanied them on a variety of expeditions and, while the students were expected to acquire knowledge from these new experiences, the outings were also agreeable. At the English College he continued to receive friends and to provide entertainment for them. The students put on plays, some of which Wiseman wrote, all lighthearted in subject-matter. Yet he was not uncritical of himself, and he noted in November 1837: 'Also I will always consider myself as I am, inferior to all, in virtue and piety, and I will industriously seek occasions of serving them in every way. . . . And as I have found by experience that in talking with my neighbours I easily allow myself to be led into uncharitable conversation, I will check myself determinately. . . .'

During his tenure as rector, Wiseman had changed, not only in outlook — he had become more human and less of the excessively dedicated scholar — but also physically. Whereas in his youth he was frail and thin, he had now become very stout, his rotundity making him look benign and somewhat like the jolly Irish priest of fiction. Frederick Faber, one of the Oxford converts, was later to say of him that 'when in full tog he looked like some Japanese God;'[15] this was hardly flattering, but, to paraphrase Lord Granville's remark on Princess Mary of Cambridge, he was a 'stout party from Rome.'

While continuing his work in Rome he did not allow himself to be deflected from his goal of returning to England. He felt that a new Pauline missionary zeal was essential in England and he hoped to establish a community to perform this service; but Rome did not yet choose to allow him to take up the task.

Wiseman was as hospitable as ever with an increasing flow of visitors, among them Gladstone and Macaulay, and they all enjoyed themselves hugely, finding Wiseman a delightful and considerate host. The nineteenth century was interested in all aspects of religion, and he often pleased his guests by his willingness to discuss theological subjects. Moreover, he was not bigoted and although firm in his beliefs, he was prepared to discuss his faith in a rational manner. Every English contact convinced him that old prejudices were dying and that his fellow countrymen would receive a revived Roman Catholicism in a charitable manner.

He was much concerned about the Catholic community in England, but was somewhat critical of the hierarchy, feeling that it was too aloof and too uninvolved with society generally. The trouble was one of national temperament and history. He, being very Roman in outlook, somehow expected more enthusiasm and a more positive policy. His views were shared by others in the papal capital and Wiseman, on more than one occasion, had to apologize to the Pope for inadequacies of his fellow countrymen. The latter, in their turn, felt Wiseman was too much of an 'ultra', too removed from the realities of the situation in England and not really able to see their position. Indeed, in April 1838 they went so far as to request that Wiseman cease to be their agent at the Holy See. The problem was the age-old controversy of Ultramontanism and Cisalpinism, Guelph versus Ghibelline. Nevertheless, by the late 1830's the Church was moving into that phase of its history when Roman authority of the type later personified by Pius IX was to become universal. As yet, however, the majority of the English Roman Catholic community were still prisoners of an earlier day when the Church had suffered active persecution; as a result, most people who were Roman Catholics preferred an inactive rôle or at least one that did not bring them too much into public view.

Concomitant with his feeling that the English Roman Catholic community needed to acquire a more active sense of itself, Wiseman was vastly interested, nay more, fascinated by the Oxford Movement. From virtually its earliest days he had felt a great sympathy for those involved and he had great hopes that it would lead to a possible conversion of much of the Anglican communion. His views on the matter were not given much support by many of his co-religionists in England, for they regarded the whole business with the gravest suspicion. Wiseman did not heed their caution, feeling it a symbol of their inadequacies, and he actively promoted

21

any and all modes of reunion. Moreover, he supported a number of Roman practices which he thought might help in the great cause. He encouraged his friends — particularly Father George Spencer, a notable convert — in their devotion to the rosary for he believed quite sincerely that through continuous prayer and the mediation of the Virgin Mary great consequences would inevitably ensue. While English Roman Catholics were not against prayer, they rather tended to regard such schemes as Wiseman proposed as being very un-English and distinctly continental, hence, as very alien to their experience. He also promoted among his own students what he called an 'apostolic spirit, where each one, besides his own special flock, takes an interest in, and exerts himself for the benefit of the entire country, according to the gifts he has received.' [16] This too did not receive universal approbation. The irrepressible and difficult Bishop Baines — a most trying man at the best of times — reckoned that at the rate converts were being received it would take two centuries to acquire a million new members, and thousands of years to bring England to recognize the pope's supremacy. Later, Baines went so far as to issue a pastoral letter to forbid what he considered to be fancy innovations, which vastly upset and disgusted Wiseman and his circle.

Wiseman had made a renewed visit to England in the summer and autumn of 1839. He established himself at Oscott where he felt particularly at home, but he also retained a base in London. He saw many friends both old and new but nothing pleased him more than 'meeting converts who came . . . to acknowledge their obligations to [him]''. When a new church was opened and consecrated at Derby, he was present and preached a sermon. In a slightly patronizing fashion he noted that the new buildings, the ceremonies and the like 'would not have done dishonour to Rome'. He visited Stalybridge also where a similar event took place, that is, a new church was consecrated with full services.

In Huddersfield the Roman Catholic community staged a great procession of clergy and laity with all the enthusiasm of continental Catholicism, and it was very unlike the more restrained tradition that characterized the English church, but he did recognize that the West Riding of Yorkshire was somewhat special and unique. He believed that in this part of the country 'bigotry . . . [was] at an end, and processions may walk the streets with no more fear of molestation than in Rome, and the priests all wear the Roman Collar and an ecclesiastical costume.' [17]

He used this visit to England to test public opinion. He lectured frequently and to sizeable audiences not only of Roman Catholics but Protestants as well. The latter received him quite cordially and

22

he felt that the old fears and prejudices held by the English Protestant communions were less rigid than in the recent past. He had great hopes that at least part of the community would ultimately accept church reunion.

After touring the midlands he returned to London where he made his headquarters until it was time to return to Rome. During his six weeks' stay in England he had travelled over 1,600 miles and delivered some ninety sermons. His experiences were such that he was more than ever convinced that he should be allowed to settle in England or, if that were not possible, at least to make frequent visits. His fame as a preacher was now general and many invitations were issued to him to come back and make another tour very shortly, but as yet he could make no promises.

When he reached the English College he could feel very satisfied with what he had done; but so much remained, and he was anxious to get back where he felt he could make a real contribution. He expressed these feelings in two letters: in one he noted, 'What good do I at Rome? Excepting in the College, nothing to the purpose; while England is in the most interesting condition, and calls for all the exertions of those that wish her well.' [18] And in another to his old friend Bagshawe, with whom he had stayed in London, he wrote: 'My just thoughts on this side of the Channel must be connected with my last on the other side. . . . When I look back at what I have got through in England, it appears to me like a dream. . . . For everything I have done has fallen wonderfully short of my desires, and everything I have acquired or effected has gone wonderfully beyond . . . my expectations.' [19]

This time he did not have long to wait, for Rome at last made up its mind about his future. During his sojourn in England, and even before, various plans had been proposed about the reorganization of the administration of the English Roman Catholic community. The Vicars Apostolic had been asked for their views, but they had been somewhat dilatory in their response; only after much prompting had they acted, and then only in a lukewarm fashion. Their replies were not uniform nor were they very constructive. On the advice of Cardinal Acton, Pope Gregory decided against the restoration of the hierarchy, as some had suggested. Instead, he proposed to increase the numbers of Vicars Apostolic but this meant that England was still only a missionary district. Much to the regret of the enthusiasts, caution had triumphed. As one part of the plan Nicholas Wiseman was named coadjutor to Bishop Walsh — now in charge of a reorganized Central District — and at the same time made President of Oscott College. At long last Wiseman was freed of his Roman obligations and could embark on a new career which to him was more significant, for he was no longer the cloistered scholar but rather the public man.

Just prior to his consecration he went to a retreat conducted by the Passionist fathers. On this occasion he had a chance to review his faith and his career. As was the case when he had sought the professorship of oriental languages, he was under great strain, both from his recent efforts and from concern for the future. Once more, doubts and anxieties overcame him; he became acutely depressed and again feared that he would go mad. But the melancholy state did not remain: after some hours of prayer and meditation he found himself calm once more, mind and soul at peace and when he went to Mass he was now sure in his purpose.

On 8 June 1840 Wiseman was consecrated as a bishop, and since England was still in *partibus infidelum* he assumed the titular see of Melipotamus. The ceremony, as was fitting, occurred in the Chapel of the English College; here he had begun his career in Rome and it was from here that he was to leave it. His first official episcopal act took place a day later when he performed the sacraments of confirmation and ordination and, while these were to be followed by many such similar occasions in the future, the initial ones had perhaps particular significance for they somehow indicated a very specific fashion what was to be his new life.

Although he had been anxious to depart from Rome, when the day finally came he was to be somewhat emotional about his leave-taking. He now regretted that the college and his friends would no longer be part of his life. However, this sentiment must be seen for what it was since only a year previously he had said that after twenty years in Rome 'I have not formed one single friendship in it. I have no family in which I am welcome. . . . [There is] . . . so little true friendship or attachments. . . .' Now it was 'a sorrowful . . . [moment]: affection clung to every old stone . . . and most of future happiness had to be invested in the mournful recollections of the past.'[21] However, *hic jacta est*. . . . He left Rome early in August 1840, travelling overland first to Venice, then to Germany, then to Belgium, finally reaching London in the first week of September.

Prior to his departure he had drawn up for himself a programme to which he was to adhere in general terms throughout his episcopal career. He proposed to emphasize the veneration given to the Virgin Mary, which for some reason he felt the English Roman Catholic community failed to do, to establish retreats, to improve the level of the clergy's education, to introduce missions, to have his special prayers such as 'the Forty Hours' and 'the Rosary' — both somewhat novel and continental — with confraternities, to hold visitations and synods, to reorganize existing administrative relationships and to introduce uniformity of clerical dress. The plan was a curious mixture of the spiritual and the practical and its priorities were in neither particular area. While the plan was ambitious, he was aware that he had little chance of success until he had the confidence of the clergy, but he hoped to gain their support for change by retreats and conferences. He was not unprepared for opposition and he recognized the difficulties which lay ahead of him, for he knew well that no change could be made without the co-operation of his colleagues, and that they were very suspicious of him and of his projects. In all fairness it must be said that he appreciated their conservatism even if he did not understand it or approve of it.

Remaining in London for less than a fortnight, he reached Oscott in mid-September 1840 where he was received with much ceremony by the staff and the boys. They and he then went in procession to the chapel where an address of welcome was read, to which he made a formal reply. For the first few weeks he was content to take little formal part in the life of the school and to consider carefully all of the many problems ahead. He hoped to organize his life in such a way as to be able to transact official business, perform his religious duties and still have time for some scholarly activities.

Oscott charmed him for it was both very similar to and very different from the English College in Rome. He soon became a great favourite with the boys with his good humour and his geniality, for he was highly approachable and obviously interested in his pupils. His colleagues on the staff were a curious *mélange*. Lord Acton, the great historian, was later to describe them as the Romans, the early converts, local clerics, tractarian converts and some Irish. He observed 'I don't think that the President amalgamated all these, or influenced them with his spirit, or gave them very definite direction',[22] but despite this, Wiseman gave the place status; he had great style himself and was a good host as well as a great trencherman. He was as hospitable at Oscott as he had been in Rome but always with a purpose as well, for he had before his eyes the vision of the conversion of the Tracterians and he believed that if they saw Catholicism as it really was their apprehensions would vanish. He had, however, no sense of money, and this was to cause problems for his rather grand manner of entertaining so lavishly was a charge on the college's expenditure, and the institution was far from rich. Moreover, as he was really concerned with Roman Catholicism in the larger sense, his career as President of Oscott did little for the college *per se*. He was adequate but not much more, for he was only partly occupied with college administration and no school makes progress in such circumstances.

Wiseman had returned to England with high hopes for the conversion of many of his fellow countrymen, but in particular he was interested in the Tractarians, whose activities he had followed closely when in Rome. Of the High Church Anglicans he wrote: 'Let us have an influx of new blood, let us have but even a small number of such men as write in the Tracts, so imbued with the spirit of the early Church; . . . let even a few such men . . . enter fully into the spirit of the Catholic religion and *we* shall be speedily reformed and England quickly converted.' [23]

Earlier he had already made some personal contact with the Oxford Movement; he had met Froude and Newman some years previously and had written articles in the *Dublin Review* on the very questions they were asking of themselves. With the appearance of Newman's *Tract #90*, which said in essence that acceptance of the Thirty Nine Articles was not inconsistent with Roman Catholic teaching, Wiseman was immensely optimistic about the future. While Newman's interpretation was not entirely correct, as Wiseman pointed out to him in a letter, it was evident that both men 'were saying "Catholic principles are true; . . . sympathize with those who hold them; true principles must lead to true conclusions," '.[24] Newman and his friends were as yet still convinced of the rightness of the Anglican position but Wiseman was confident that ultimately they would be forced to abandon their Protestantism and come over to Rome.

Throughout the years 1841–42, Wiseman and the Tractarians went through a series of motions which can be somewhat likened to the Lobsters' Quadrille. Ralph Waldo Sibthorpe, a Fellow of Magdalen College, Oxford, joined the Catholic Church in 1841 and his adherence was the occasion for much joy to Wiseman: this did not last long, however, as Sibthorpe recanted shortly thereafter. Some years later though, he rejoined the Roman Catholic Church. Sibthorpe's defection caused Wiseman's critics to take a very high line of 'we told you so'. There were others, such as Bernard Smith and Charles Seager, who were converted, but they were less impetuous in their actions, being more thoughtful once they had resolved to become Roman Catholics.

Yet his whole time was not occupied with the Tractarians however, for he continued to preside at Oscott and to perform episcopal functions when required: however, since he did not have a regular see, these duties were far from onerous. As can readily be understood, he was much concerned about Ireland, and while sympathetic to the distresses of the Irish people he had his reservations about the activities of O'Connell and the Repeal Association, especially so when it held meetings on Sundays, but he was not immune from the contemporary attitudes towards the sabbath, and long residence in Rome had failed to extinguish a puritanical spirit. His hospitality at Oscott continued on a considerable scale, and visitors came in shoals. Wiseman, although a simple person, essentially could not resist a lord and he was so enraptured by a visit from the Comte de Chambord that he even wrote a poem — a very feeble effort — full of high sentiment.

To escape from the harshness of an English winter he went to Spain in 1844. Landing first at Cadiz he went on to make his first visit in forty years to his birthplace, Seville; here he was a guest of a relative named Stanley. He was given a warm welcome by everyone, many of whom remembered his parents. Everything pleased him 'except the abominable treatment of the Church by the secular power in every succeeding government of Spain since '21.' [25] He stayed in Seville for a week, travelled to Cordova, Granada and Malaga before returning to Cadiz to re-embark for England. His holiday did much to raise his spirits, and to restore his health; once again he was ready for the fray.

Soon after he returned home, William Ward, another of the Tractarians, published his *The Ideal of a Christian Church*. This book produced a violent reaction, more indeed than had Newman's *Tract ♯90*, for its author, officially an Anglican, had stated that he accepted Roman Catholic doctrine completely. The upshot was that in February 1845 Ward was deprived of his degrees by Convocation at Oxford. At the same time efforts to condemn *Tract ♯90* were defeated when the Proctors used their power of veto. Newman thus managed to escape official censure, but it was simply a matter of time before his enemies would find cause to condemn him too. Ward and his wife became Roman Catholics in the following June, but Newman still did nothing.

In order to ascertain more specifically what Newman's position was, Wiseman sent an emissary to Littlemore. Bernard Smith, once Newman's curate, who made the visit, learned nothing official: but in the evening, Newman appeared in grey trousers. Smith appreciated the gesture, for it was evident that Newman no longer thought of himself as an Anglican clergyman; but he still did not take the final step. In September two of his dearest friends left Littlemore and became Roman Catholics and another announced that it was his intention to follow them. Increasingly isolated but now sure of himself, Newman finally made up his mind and on 8 October 1845 he too became a Roman Catholic.

Wiseman was delighted by Newman's conversion. It was the

climax of all that he had hoped and prayed for. He could now turn on his detractors and say with certainty that he had been right in his anticipations. When the two men met at the end of October 1845, it was not a rapturous occasion but quiet and somewhat melancholy. Wiseman was not to be cheated of his triumph and Newman, in the company of nine other former Anglican clerics was confirmed by Wiseman on 1 November 1845. The new converts soon departed, but he was now actively promoting a project whereby Newman and his friends would reside permanently at Oscott. Newman was seemingly less enthusiastic than Wiseman, and was disinclined at this juncture to give a definite answer. Moreover, he wanted to finish writing his book *Essay on Development*.

Of course Newman was not the only convert, but he was certainly the most famous. Littlemore had been the home for some, while others were from aristocratic and landed families; but they were all prominent in one way or another. Moreover, unlike the case of poor Sibthorpe, none recanted and to its enemies, the Anglican Church was almost like a wounded animal in its death throes; its powers of recovery, however, were proved to be stronger than they appeared to be.

Wiseman was at once confronted with a very real problem, namely, how to meld the converts and the 'old' Catholics into a coherent whole. He was well aware of the difficulties. Most immediate was his concern to find occupations for the converts. The celibates were easy — they could become priests, either seculars or regulars — but the married men were often near to starvation since their families tended to shun them completely and their future was bleak indeed. Wiseman tried to employ as many as possible in various ways on the *Dublin Review* and some became regular contributors: but not all could be so readily accommodated.

Feelings of spiritual elation continued, but at the same time his physical state declined; it seems likely that he had overexerted himself in the last few years, and inevitably, once the initial enthusiasm over the success of his policies lessened, there was a natural let-down. Moreover, throughout his whole life he was prone to fits of depression and this present situation was no novelty. He needed a cause to sustain him but it was not immediately that he found one. For the moment more mundane tasks were at hand and the most immediate was the settlement of the converts.

Following the election of Pius IX in 1846 it seemed sensible to Wiseman that he should revive the project of the restoration of the hierarchy. The old system of Vicars Apostolic had worked well enough in the past when the Roman Catholic community was either actively persecuted or at least subject to the Penal Laws; but the situation was now different. While the whole arrangement had been modified in 1840, the English were still really outside the regular Roman Catholic establishment.

Wiseman went off to Rome in July 1847 to put before the new Pope his request that the hierarchy be established or rather re-established. Not only did he believe that this restoration was important for social reasons, but also because canon law did not apply under the present system and no local synods were possible to resolve problems. Wiseman did not have unanimous support for his project either in England or in Rome; Cardinal Acton, at that time the only English Cardinal and the official spokesman for English interests, thought the plan premature and he advised caution. Wiseman at least managed to get a hearing, but before anything was done, domestic political problems in the papal states intervened.

Pius IX had given some encouragement to liberal sentiment in Italy and had promoted reforms in his own territories. To continue these policies he required the active support of not only like-minded Italians but of others elsewhere. Moreover, following the Austrian occupation of Ferrara in the summer of 1847 the situation became very complicated indeed. In order to gain British approbation for his policies, Pius IX sent his man back to London in late August to put his case before Palmerston.

Wiseman returned to the British capital a fortnight later and called on the Foreign Secretary: but the latter was away from his office. Wiseman then wrote a brief to Palmerston outlining the situation. He described the principal reforms enacted by Pius IX — all in accord with the suggestions contained in the notes submitted by the Great Powers in 1831 — and he explained the general state of the political parties, the plot of 16 July and the action of the Austrian and Neapolitan governments. He also noted that France seemed inclined to support the more conservative forces. Wiseman called on Russell's government, and Palmerston in particular, to assist the papacy in its struggle against Austria and Metternich and in so doing help promote Italian freedom. Such an appeal found Palmerston sympathetic and Lord Minto went out to Italy as a sort of unofficial emissary; unfortunately his mission did not accomplish its real purpose for events moved too rapidly and the revolution of 1848 overtook them all. Pius IX fled from Rome, the radicals took power for some months and when the Pope did return in 1850 it was not as a liberal but as a conservative.

Meanwhile the great project for the hierarchy continued to receive sympathetic attention in Rome. Cardinal Acton died in 1847 and a major obstacle was thereby removed. The British government, who had been consulted when a hierarchy was established in Australia and in Upper Canada, seemed to be totally disinterested. Moreover, in August 1848 Lord John Russell, the Prime Minister, had stated in parliament that papal authority over the Roman Catholic Church in England was not at that time subject to any control. While he did not give his formal approval for the establishment of a Roman Catholic episcopate he did not see, except by some new law, how the Pope's power could be limited and he did not think it wise to prevent the Pope from being able to act as he chose. Wiseman had once more come back to England and Ullathorne had taken his place in Rome. The matter was settled but not put into effect prior to Pius IX's flight to Gaeta.

For the interim, Wiseman had been appointed Pro-Vicar Apostolic of London upon his return and in the spring of the next year he had assumed office *in plentitudo potestas*. From the start he was very busy. One outward sign of the changed situation since 1829 was the opening of St. George's Church in Southwark. In this instance fourteen bishops and 240 priests were present, and the *Illustrated London News* even sent an artist to do some drawings so that its readers would have an idea of the occasion. Everywhere Wiseman was introducing more and more 'Roman' customs, including what he called 'religious education' meaning 'full reverence to the Saints, and interest concerning them.' [26] These practices were somewhat alien to the old English spirit but were warmly supported by the enthusiastic converts. He reported on a case of faith healing through the use of a relic of St. Philomena (what would he have thought of the decree abolishing her, one wonders?) and he was on the lookout for relics all the time. He felt the promotion of the saints had a 'good effect on devotion, by softening some of our rigidness of mind on such subjects; this would be truly promoting a *cultus*, which forms part of the Catholic system, towards the servants of God.' [27] If the Protestants had known of these activities they would have been even more convinced of the iniquities of Catholicism; moreover, if Wiseman had realized it, his 'Romanism' was at variance with English life and it would help to explain the outburst against him in 1850.

During the summer of 1849 he went down to Eastbourne for a brief holiday, but he did not neglect his work and used his sojourn by the sea-side to catch up on his correspondence. On this occasion he wrote something over one hundred letters, but he was not good at organizing his paper work and he often failed to reply to correspondents for long periods thus seeming to be indifferent to his friends. While such was not the case, it sometimes caused unnecessary complications and led to both unhappiness and real distress.

Wiseman's accomplishments in his first year of office were very considerable. He had set up seven new monastic communities and three convents, opened two orphanages, created a Catholic grammar school, organized eleven missions and arranged for retreats to be held in London in various sections of the city. His policies were still criticized, but he recognized at this time that the old 'Gallican spirit' died hard, and that the opposition still existed. He often felt very much alone and once more was subject to fits of depression. He was somewhat isolated, true; but he was supported enthusiastically by the converts. However, he needed the approbation of the whole Catholic community to feel really secure.

His work had been appreciated by his ecclesiastical superiors, however, and in May 1850 he was informed by Cardinal Antonelli that Pius IX intended to give him a red hat with the consistory to occur in September, and he was requested to attend. Wiseman had wanted to lead the English episcopate but now it appeared that Rome had other plans. He felt that the Vatican did not understand how much was still to be done, but he was an obedient son of the Church and despite personal anguish, to Rome he would go. His interpretation of the situation was that the Pope had another candidate to become the head of the Church in England. While he recognized that he was being honoured he certainly did not now wish to live in Rome permanently.

When he left London in mid-August he believed that he was leaving England for ever. Many of his co-religionists were dismayed, but others were probably much less so for his activist policies were displeasing so many. Even in the midst of all of his preparations he continued to be as concerned with his beloved *Dublin Review* — he was still an editor — and on the journey even wrote to his colleagues about a forthcoming article.

His journey to Rome took three weeks; he was very sad when he had embarked for he was going with reluctance, but doing so as the result of the papal command. On his trip he visited Paris where he stayed two days — part of the time was spent in correcting a sermon for the publisher — and went on to Italy later in the month where he had a couple of days with his sister who had married a member of the Italian nobility. He finally reached Rome in September. Upon his arrival he was immediately received in private audience by the Pope, and was informed that he was not to be exiled from England after all as it had been decided that he was not only to become a cardinal but also an archbishop and the head of the newly re-established hierarchy. At a second meeting with Pius IX the English episcopate was formally set up, but the brief announcing this fact was not published until early in October.

31

While waiting for the consistory to occur and for the announcement by Pius IX about the hierarchy, Wiseman busied himself visiting old friends and receiving others at his residence. At the end of September he was formally raised to the rank of Prince of the Church and named Cardinal Priest of St. Pudentiana. Receptions followed; all of this was very grand and somewhat expensive too — the fees alone were £500 — and he had to bear the cost of the receptions as well. However, the Vatican promised him extra funds to cover his increased expenses which made things somewhat easier.

For once, Wiseman did not intend to linger in Rome on this occasion. He sent a formal communication to England announcing that the hierarchy had been re-established. Naturally, he was much elated; gone was the depression of a few months earlier. He left Rome in the middle of October, went north to Florence and four days later was received by the Grand Duke of Tuscany at Sienna in considerable state; a large reception followed the next night, and after a week's stay he went on to Bologna, to Venice and then by train to Vienna. He reached the imperial capital at the end of the month, and dined with Emperor Francis Joseph on All Saints' Day. Thus far everything was as it should be: but nemesis was at hand.

On 3 November the blow fell. As he said, 'I was . . . reading my *Times*,[28] when I received a rude shock as I saw my name in the leading article.'[29] The article, which had been printed on 14 October, began harmlessly enough, saying that it was no surprise that Wiseman had become a cardinal as he was learned and able; but to conjoin this promotion with the creation of the archiepiscopal see of Westminster was, in the opinion of *The Times*, an act of stupidity and presumption. Wiseman would receive that just disapprobation of the English public which he deserved. In its leader *The Times* was deliberately reviving all of the anti-Catholicism latent in England. This situation was to be made worse when Wiseman's own *Pastoral* was published for it appeared to be very extreme in its claims.

He very sensibly decided that the only solution was to cope directly with the problems that had been raised. As Newman later remarked, 'I was not prepared for such a display of vigour, power, judgment, sustained energy. . . .'[30] First Wiseman proceeded to write to Russell, the Prime Minister: in his letter he began by discussing the question of an English diplomatic mission to Rome and reported that the Vatican would be delighted to receive an emissary from Britain. This information was in response to a query he had been asked earlier. He continued by affirming that in

32

his last interview with the Prime Minister he had sincerely believed that he would not be returning to England. Turning to the question of the hierarchy he observed that three years earlier Lord Minto had actually seen the papal brief on the matter, but that no final decision had been taken at that time as other events, more pressing, had intervened. He further stated that the creation of an archiepiscopal see had nothing to do with policies or private pique on the part of Pius IX. He declared that his office was ecclesiastical only: 'I have no secular or temporal delegation whatever; that my duties will be what they have ever been, to promote the morality of those committed to my charge, especially the masses of our poor; and to keep up those feelings of goodwill and friendly inter-communion between Catholics and their fellow countrymen which I flatter myself I have been the means of somewhat improving.' [31] In his conclusion he observed that he hoped that the public would soon comprehend that the decision only involved the Roman Catholic community and was designed for the better government of their Church.

Following the dispatch of his letter Wiseman could only await developments. He left Vienna, went on to Cologne where he stayed only briefly and then to Bruges. At this stage Russell took no action and appeared to have accepted Wiseman's view that the newly founded hierarchy was purely a sectarian question: but the situation was to change radically over the next month; the long pastoral letter was read in all Roman Catholic churches on 20 October and elsewhere a week later. On 29 October it was published in full in *The Times*. Its style and tone, which was naturally enough fulsome and joyous, was interpreted by the editor of *The Times* to be arrant presumption. England restored to its place indeed! Wiseman to rule the home counties! Queen Victoria could well enquire: 'Am I Queen of England or am I not?' [32] and then the grand finale of 'given out of the Flaminian Gate of Rome': pure papal aggression. The publication of the pastoral letter revived all the anti-Catholic and 'no-popery' sentiment. Even some Roman Catholics were perturbed, not so much at the restoration of the hierarchy but at the rather exuberant way of announcing it.

The Prime Minister now took a step which aggravated the situation still further; he wrote a letter to the Bishop of Durham saying that he was indignant that Pius IX had been so insolent as to act as he had done. While he did not say he thought it improper for an episcopate to be established by the Roman Catholic Church, he repudiated papal claims to supremacy in England, declaring such action violated statutes of Henry VIII and Elizabeth I. Pursuing this line of argument he continued that no Pope could be permitted

33

'to impose a foreign yoke upon our minds and consciences. No foreign prince or potentate will be permitted to fasten his fetters upon a nation which has so long and so nobly vindicated its right to freedom of opinion, civil, political, and religious.' He repeated his views in an address in the Guildhall and his colleague Lord Truro, the Lord Chancellor took a similar position saying: 'Under our feet we'll stamp the Cardinal's hat, in spite of Pope or dignities of Church.' [33] Following these outbursts from individuals who ought to have been more circumspect, further articles and letters continued to appear in *The Times*, effigies of both Wiseman and Pius IX were paraded and then burned — it was all very convenient coming so close to Guy Fawkes Night — Catholic clerics were attacked, their churches were stoned, numerous public meetings were held and the Anglican bishops — virtually en bloc — deplored the papal decision on the hierarchy as an 'unwarrantable insult.'

Wiseman's own friends thought that he would be sensible to stay on the continent until the situation calmed down: but they did not know their man. On receiving all of this information he became more determined to press on. He reached London on 11 November, stayed initially with the Bagshawe family and then moved to a residence near St. George's Church in Southwark. Even before landing in England he had already begun to prepare his reply. The Vicar General — the same Father Whitty who had published the *Pastoral* as instructed — was dumbfounded when Wiseman said that he believed he was writing something which would dampen down the excitement. As Whitty remarked to him, 'Well, you are indeed a sanguine man to expect that yours or *any* writing can calm this storm.' [34]

He had soon completed his response to Russell and the other critics. It was published in pamphlet form on 19 November and printed verbatim the next day in *The Times*. In his statement Wiseman was very forthright and did not hesitate to give his opinions of Russell and Truro. Moreover, he believed that if people understood the situation properly they would be inclined to give him a fair-minded decision. He began his statement by refuting the implied charge that the Roman Catholics were disloyal. Certainly they denied royal supremacy in matters of religion but so did the many others whose patriotism was never in question. He stated plainly that a proper episcopal establishment was essential for the good government of the Roman Catholic Church and that new bishops would not infringe on the rights of their Anglican colleagues. He also pointed out that the Church of England had created bishoprics outside England and that nobody felt the Queen was exceeding her authority. He ended his *Appeal*, and this is really the only part which might be said to reflect the more emotional aspect of Wiseman's nature, by declaring that his 'Westminster' was the slums of the city where the sad, the lonely, the diseased, and the poor resided and that he did not intend to obtrude himself upon the Dean and Chapter of Westminster Abbey or upon Parliament.

The reaction was he he had predicted; some 30,000 copies of the pamphlet were sold almost overnight and not only to Roman Catholics. The press generally agreed that he had put his case well and had proved that the restoration of the hierarchy was only an internal matter for the Roman Catholics. Very quickly it was apparent to most people that no attack on England was meant and that there was really no 'papal aggression.' *The Times*, still huffing and puffing, gradually calmned down. Moreover, Russell, the Prime Minister, was made to look very foolish because he and his government had accepted Roman Catholic prelates in Ireland and what, it could be asked, was the difference between them and Wiseman and his colleagues?

Not all of his fellow Roman Catholics supported Wiseman though; two prominent peers sided with the government. Lord Beaumont thought, for rather obscure reasons, that the acceptance of the hierarchy would imperil Roman Catholics' rights as citizens, and the Duke of Norfolk commented 'that ultramontane opinions are totally incompatible with allegiance to our Sovereign and with our Constitution.' [35] They expressed their views publicly but were the only ones to do so, though others may well have had their private reservations. On the whole, however, Roman Catholic unity was complete. Even the Queen, who earlier had been incensed, had now been restored to a more calm view of the situation though Russell continued to remain obdurate and persisted in introducing his 'Ecclesiastical Titles Bill' in February. The text, in simple terms, denied the right of anyone to assume titles to episcopal sees in Great Britain and fined anyone who did £100. It became law in August but it was really dead from the moment of its enactment and it was repealed a generation later. However, it did indicate that despite the most rational explanation of Pius IX's policy, many Englishmen were still highly suspicious of Rome.

Hardly had this crisis ended than a new one began. In an article in the *Dublin Review* Wiseman had attacked a man named Achilli, a lapsed Roman Catholic cleric. Newman had also been critical of him and these attacks on Achilli's probity made him appear to many Protestants to be a much maligned man. In due course Achilli proceeded to sue Newman for libel; the latter lost his case, in part because Wiseman was unable to find the original papers upon which his own article in the *Dublin Review* was based. *The Times* felt the whole thing a travesty of justice — the judge had been very biassed — and made a real *amende honorable* for its earlier attacks on Roman Catholics. Newman appealed, the case was heard anew, and he lost again, though his damages were negligible. Wiseman raised money to help pay Newman's costs but the whole affair was most unfortunate; indeed he was extremely culpable for allowing Newman to be placed in such an untenable position. It was, moreover, another indication of the somewhat disorganized way in which Wiseman tended to operate because he did not keep his notes and records in as precise a manner as a man in his position should have done.

In April 1851 Henry Edward Manning became a Roman Catholic; he was soon ordained to the priesthood and went to Rome where he remained for three years. Wiseman, as can be imagined, was delighted with his new convert. Later, Manning was to become Wiseman's greatest protégé and his ultimate successor. Manning was not alone in this second wave of conversions, and Wiseman felt all the more optimistic for the future.

Once the excitement over the restoration of the hierarchy disappeared, Wiseman's life returned to its more accustomed pattern. He held his first synod at Oscott in the summer of 1852. Generally speaking he had his own way on most matters but there were still disagreements between the adherents of the more traditional English Roman Catholic attitudes and the ultramontanism of the converts. In fact he personally sympathized with the latter, but at the same time he realized he would have to work hard to harmonize the two traditions. To put his views forward to a larger public, he gave numerous lectures which were well attended. He also spoke on non-theological subjects — this was very much in the spirit of the age — and these lectures were popular. Wiseman, like his contemporaries, was willing to be the instant expert on all manner of things hoping thereby to raise the general educational level of society.

The years 1852 and 1853 saw no diminution in the disagreements between the various factions in the Roman Catholic community. In all of these Wiseman attempted to mediate, and in all his attempts he failed. The result was that he had another attack of melancholia. Rome was very unhelpful, for the Vatican authorities were all extreme papalists and were not sympathetic to those who sought to preserve the older traditions of what was really a form of Gallicanism. In an effort to improve his spirits and at the same time to try and get the situation in England more fully understood Wiseman went to Rome in the autumn of 1853. On his way he

36

visited Amiens and was present at a great religious ceremony which, with his love of pageantry, was very much to his liking. Both Napoleon III and his wife were in the congregation and following the ceremonies he was presented to the Empress. All these junketings improved his spirits. He stayed in Paris for a few days before going to Rome where he was most cordially received by Monsignor Talbot, the Pope's private confidant, and by Cardinal Antonelli, the Secretary of State. He had an audience with Pius IX, attended a consistory and dined in state with the Grand Duke of Tuscany — he was very fond of royals. Everything in the papal capital pleased him, for as he observed to his old friend Bagshawe: 'Personally, I have already received benefits in health and spirits, for I was losing both fast before I left England. But how different I find things here, and how truly I am at once at home among those who can understand my conduct and know my principles and motives, and do not by rule misjudge me.'

While in Rome Wiseman remembered his friends; Ward was made a Doctor of Philosophy and Faber became a Doctor of Divinity; he failed, however, to get a titular bishopric for Newman. He was in no great hurry to return to England; indeed, his lengthy sojourn in Rome gave rise to rumours that he was about to retire to Italy permanently, but he quite firmly denied that there was any such plan afoot for it was his fixed intention to return to London in the spring to resume his duties. While he was much occupied with official business he also made a start on his novel *Fabiola*. It was a pleasant activity which required less effort than scholarship and it amused him to try his hand at fiction. Moreover, such a novel would serve to spread the true Christian message in another guise and to an audience not prone to read theology. His holiday in Italy thoroughly restored his morale and he was ready to take on his many tasks that awaited him in England.

It was a good thing that he was in such a positive mood, for a new crisis awaited him. It was another of those controversies between the old traditions and the new. Father Boyle who had been at Islington felt aggrieved because he thought Wiseman had unjustly dispossessed him of his curacy even though compensation had been given him for personal expenditures and the like. As a result, Boyle and a colleague wrote a series of articles in a French journal attacking Wiseman and all of his works. To these articles Wiseman replied by a letter which was ultimately reproduced in translation in *The Tablet*. Wiseman in his reply had been in top form — he was always good in controversy — and set out the facts as he understood them. Boyle was furious and proceeded to sue his superior for libel; the issue really turned on the use of the word

37

renvoyé which *The Tablet* had mistranslated as 'expelled', while more properly it should have been 'discharged'. Initially, Wiseman won, but on appeal the decision was reversed and the cardinal was required to pay £1,000 damages. This time he appealed and another trial was ordered; Boyle capitulated and in declining to pursue the case forfeited all claim. Wiseman, although ultimately victorious, did not really win for the public regarded the whole business as a most disagreeable affair. Boyle was thought to be the victim of persecution, which he was not, and Wiseman was seen as a sort of bully who could win because he had money for legal counsel. Irreparable damage was done and the Catholics did not have a particularly good image in England.

Between the first and second trial he calmly went to the country and stayed in Yorkshire. While there he spent much of the time working on the manuscript of his novel *Fabiola*, the text of which was completed by September; the book appeared later in the year and was a great success. Not surprisingly, he was delighted by the number of copies sold. While it was not noticed by the literary reviewers, the public at large vastly enjoyed it. It was to be translated into a number of European languages and to be reprinted in numerous editions.

He made another trip to Rome in the late autumn, staying in Italy again over the winter. He enjoyed all of the pageantry of the Vatican and all of the esteem which was his as a Prince of the Church. Once more he felt refreshed and restored when he went back to England. Moreover, his triumph over Boyle and other traducers gave him greater confidence for the future.

His personal enthusiasms always tended to over-ride political realities. He was an ardent Bonapartist: he had become acquainted with Napoleon years ago in Rome and he regarded the emperor as the special protector of the Holy See. Therefore, when the Prince Imperial was born in the spring of 1855 he had a special *Te Deum* sung, an action which did not endear him to many of his fellow Catholics who were strongly legitimist in sentiment, nor to many of his fellow countrymen who still distrusted Napoleon despite the fact that he was their ally against the Russians.

The English had many curious attitudes about the Pope. For example, a number of them took considerable umbrage over the signing of a concordat between Rome and Austria which was none of their affair, but they persisted in seeing it as some devious papist plot to dominate Europe. Wiseman decided to use the occasion to deliver yet another series of public lectures to educate his countrymen. He developed his theme historically and concluded with an analysis of the concordat itself. He later published the

38

lectures, thereby reaching a wider audience, and while the more bigoted anti-papists were not to be convinced, many others who read the lectures understood more fully what the concordat actually attempted to do.

Once again his general physical state declined and he found himself unable to cope with the routine affairs of his archdiocese. Inevitably such a situation created some real difficulties. To escape from boredom and to try and recover his health, he took a continental holiday in the summer of 1856. Upon his return he found that once more a row had broken out between the converts and the conservatives, and he began to feel that he was never to have any peace. There were faults on both sides; as was not unusual the converts were often somewhat zealous in their devotions and to the older English Catholic families they showed an excess enthusiasm which was thoroughly alien. However, Wiseman did not see it that way; his own sympathies were with the converts and to him enthusiasm was an outward manifestation of faith, and, being an enthusiast himself, a sign of grace. In addition, the traditional Catholics were made increasingly irritated when the intellectual journal *The Rambler* virtually said they were a lot of uneducated bumpkins. On this matter he very wisely took the position that this last was controversy for the sake of controversy and said so in the *Dublin Review*. Instead, he strongly advocated that they should all join in for a common purpose, insisting that the ultimate cause was more important than a lot of petty jealousies and that if all would follow his advice there would be no problems. The difficulty was that not all were prepared to be guided by his personal opinions.

It was clear that in order to do battle on all fronts — intellectual, moral, social and religious — he felt he needed aid in the form of a coadjutor. His friend and confidant Monsignor Talbot in Rome proposed an auxiliary rather than a coadjutor because an auxiliary was an inferior and removable, while a coadjutor was a co-equal with guaranteed rights of succession. Wiseman was convinced that a coadjutor was necessary and had his own candidate, George Errington, his old school friend and fellow student in Rome. He and Errington had been associates throughout their lives; they would make a good team. Wiseman's enthusiasm, his extrovert personality, his support of ultramontanism and his inefficiency were a contrast to Errington's coolness, his conservatism and his orderly mind. Wiseman got his way, Rome agreed and Errington was appointed; but the latter had doubts about the wisdom of it all and, as it turned out, his doubts were fully justified.

In an attempt to define areas of responsibility, Errington was given charge of diocesan administration but in fact his authority was constantly being undermined by Wiseman's interference. Errington was strict, Wiseman was lenient; thus problems were bound to ensue. While there were difficulties of a minor sort from the outset, the first major controversy was over Ward. Errington disliked his ideas and methods of teaching and as a result Ward resigned. Wiseman was much distressed for he had appointed Ward and liked him as a man, with the result that he decided not to accept Ward's resignation so that Errington's position was somewhat undermined. It quickly became evident that the cardinal had really relinquished none of his authority, despite the appointment of Errington.

Errington, who was most perceptive, soon felt he did not have Wiseman's personal confidence and decided the best thing might well be for Rome to replace him as soon as was convenient. Wiseman did not favour such a radical course of action; he was optimistic and felt that with time everything would be happily resolved. Errington was unconvinced and took the drastic step of writing to Talbot and soliciting his advice; saying '. . . you can offer at once to the Holy Father my resignation, and readiness for such other work as may seem to him more proper,' [36] but this offer was rejected. However, it would have been better ultimately if Errington's proposal had been accepted.

Because of Rome's decision, Errington agreed to remain. However, Talbot remonstrated with Wiseman for his interference and pointed out what would be the consequence if Errington did leave. For once, Talbot did not support his friend, recognizing that he had been very unfair in his treatment of his coadjutor. Although the immediate crisis was resolved, Errington was now less secure in Wiseman's regard and suspicions on both sides continued. To add to the problem it was during this period of tension that Manning was emerging as Wiseman's protégé. Wiseman arranged for the latter to do missionary work in London and requested Errington's help as Manning's immediate superior. Errington declined to assist since he suspected that Manning and the Oblates of St. Charles would be too independent. To add to the problem, and obviously on Wiseman's solicitations, Pius IX named Manning a Canon of Westminster and Provost of the Cathedral.

Just as Errington suspected, difficulties arose soon enough and relations between Manning and himself rapidly deteriorated. On every occasion Manning had the cardinal's ear and got his own way on all matters. It was a disagreement over the regulations concerning the Oblates of St. Charles that led to a real confrontation. Wiseman interfered and gave his total support to Manning; Errington took a contrary position with the result that the cardinal accused his coadjutor of being like a legal counsel for the opposition and in the attempt to solve these new difficulties both sides appealed to Rome. With Errington openly opposed to his policies, Wiseman now began to think seriously about removing him, but to his dismay he found the whole cathedral chapter against him, and this put him into an acute depression. Even his secretary of twenty years, Monsignor Searle, sided with the chapter and although the cardinal and Searle were not to separate, the old familiarity was gone. Wiseman wrote to Rome giving his account of the situation, insisting that the Oblates had acted entirely with his permission but concurrently, Errington had written to the Vatican presenting the other side of the case.

In an attempt to escape from the turmoil and suspicion, he made a trip to Ireland. With him was his friend Monsignor Talbot, fresh from Rome, and undoubtedly many confidences were exchanged. The episcopal party arrived late in August and Wiseman was received with enthusiasm; from his point of view the whole excursion was a series of triumphs. He visited Dublin, dined at the Mansion House, toured the city, and everywhere he was given a cordial reception, by Protestants as well as Roman Catholics. As usual he delivered a number of sermons and lectures all of which were rapturously applauded. He stayed in Ireland for three weeks and his sojourn in the country was fully described in a four hundred page book called *Cardinal Wiseman's Tour in Ireland*. On his return to London he gave a full report of his activities in still another public lecture in early November to a large and appreciative audience; he obviously needed this form of approbation to reassure him.

The struggle between the chapter as supported by Errington on the one hand and the Oblates supported by Wiseman on the other continued unabated. Papers, documents, reports and letters were despatched to Rome in large quantities and the participants on both sides went off to present their case to the Pope with the result that relations between Wiseman and Errington became colder than ever. Although Piux IX sympathized with Wiseman in his trials he also knew that some of the difficulties arose from Wiseman's own nature. For the moment the Pope decided that the English could solve their own problems; if they succeeded they would have learned a good lesson in local responsibility. Besides, the Vatican was somewhat irritated with the succession of domestic quarrels. However, on the problem of the relationship between Wiseman and Errington, it is evident that Pope Pius IX took a very personal interest. He was fond of Wiseman and he appreciated Errington, but he was personally an ultramontanist and in the conflict of traditions Wiseman represented the Pope's own position. Pius was not an unfeeling man, and through the channel of the ubiquitous Monsignor Talbot, Errington was offered the Archiepiscopal See of Trinidad. This post was one that Errington himself had considered earlier but had not accepted. Unfortunately, instead of merely acting as emissary Talbot proceeded to take sides, openly accusing Errington of being disloyal and opposed to Wiseman's ultramontanist policies.

Naturally Errington was most hurt by the charges, took very real umbrage and denied them. To add to the complications, Talbot now somewhat belatedly attempted to explain himself and replied that he had only meant that Errington and Wiseman were not in sympathy, asserting that both were good sons of the Church but that the cardinal's views represented papal policy and hence he would be supported both publicly and privately. Errington now became very obstinate and obdurately refused to comply with Talbot's request that the business be arranged 'as quietly as possible and to prevent the scandal of having recourse to more rigorous measures.' [37]

Meanwhile, Wiseman was far from being victorious either, for at the synod held in the summer he was roundly defeated, with Errington and his supporters in the chapter declining to make any concessions. Interestingly enough, there is very real evidence that the Vatican was not at all convinced that Wiseman's policy had been right, but it was far from pleased with Errington's rôle in organizing the opposition and the Pope intended to support his personal friend. Wiseman decided that it was only in Rome itself that he would get his way, for he had received several amiable communications from Pius IX. Moreover, Talbot in other letters confirmed also that he would be given a most cordial welcome the moment that he arrived.

As in the past — and one wonders if the cause was not psychosomatic — he now fell into a state of acute depression, followed by a mild heart attack: this made him more gloomy than ever. Nevertheless, he was determined to go to Rome and, accompanied by Monsignor Searle — despite the latter's championing of Errington's cause — he arrived in December. Errington had also come to the conclusion that he too could only receive a fair hearing from the Pope himself and consequently he reached Rome at about the same time as Wiseman. The final scene of the drama had begun.

Naturally, as always, Wiseman lodged in his old rooms in the English College. (One wonders what the incumbent rector thought of his distinguished guest assuming such proprietary rights.) The journey had not unduly fatigued him, for he prided himself on being a good sailor when the sea was rough; but once in Rome, his ill-health returned and he could hardly get about. After hearing the views of the various protagonists on the lesser issues, such as the problems with Bishop Grant's financial administration and the various difficulties ensuing from the synod's action over the Oblates of St. Charles, the Pope, while finding that Wiseman had over-stepped his authority in some instances, in general gave his total approval of the latter's policies and decisions. All of this vastly encouraged Wiseman and his gloominess soon vanished. He went about Rome in a very happy mood, visited old friends and old places with the enthusiasm of a tourist making his first trip to the city. Everyone gave him a friendly reception. However, the problem of how to solve the situation about Errington without a scandal meant that everyone was being cautious.

Wiseman was joined by Manning in the new year. He was glad to have the support of his protégé, for whom he had sacrificed so much. The two men knew that the final reckoning could not be far off and that they had to be prepared to defend their positions; for although the Vatican thus far had seemed to be inclined in their favour, there was no absolute guarantee that the ultimate decision would result in Errington's removal from office.

Pius IX was a kindly man who did not like being unpleasant, and hated personal quarrels. In an attempt to resolve the crisis, he tried to persuade Archbishop Errington to resign, and almost begged him to do so. Somewhat self-righteously Errington declared he would accept dismissal but he would not resign to make things easier for his opponents. Somewhat irritated, the Pope agreed to the formation of a special commission with both parties submitting their cases in writing. Following the writing of his brief, Wiseman left Rome and went off on a holiday. Once more his depressions had returned — did he fear defeat? — but a couple of months of leisure restored his spirits. He was back in Rome by June, again became ill, this time seriously, required an operation and careful nursing, but by midsummer he was on the mend.

In the meantime, the Errington case had been settled. The papal commission formally decided that Errington had to go. Once again Pius IX tried to persuade him to resign but, as before, he declined to be co-operative, with the result that on 22 July 1860, he was formally deprived of his coadjutorship. It was a sad end to so many hopes; of course, Errington had really brought much of it upon himself but at the same time his only real problem had been that he would not work with Wiseman and Manning. Errington refused ever to accept any other employment, and he died a quarter of a century later, having spent the intervening years teaching theology at Prior Park — the same place where Wiseman had many years earlier hoped to head a special Roman Catholic university. In a mood of triumph Wiseman returned to England. But the general state of his health was not good; the recent difficulties had been a great strain. However, he was determined not to surrender either to his opponents in the chapter nor to the exigencies of his weakened physical condition.

In Wiseman's immediate circle both of friends and advisors Manning became more and more prominent; but the cardinal was unwilling, both for political and personal reasons, to ask that Manning be named coadjutor. He probably hoped that Manning would be his successor, but hoped also this would be the decision of Rome and not through his actions. Nevertheless he used him as an agent and confidant, for the two men had common aims, though their methods of acting and thinking were very different. On one occasion Wiseman described Manning as 'a parson from the crown of his head to the soles of his feet.' But Manning got things done: he was careful and businesslike and did not worry the Cardinal — unlike his secretary Monsignor Searle whose fussiness irritated his employer. Manning was cool, self-contained and certain; Wiseman was none of these things. In fact Manning had many of Errington's characteristics but with much greater political finesse. In the last years, Wiseman and Manning did complement each other and the latter was more than willing to assume the duller aspects of ecclesiastical business both in London and in Rome on Wiseman's behalf. However, the cardinal archbishop continued to participate in things which interested him. He supported the creation of a scholarly society, the Academia, and he hoped that it would concern itself with a great variety of problems and ideas. Wiseman, whatever his faults, saw 'Catholic' in the widest sense; after his death the Academia became rather more narrow and an agent of extreme ultramontanist ideas.

Because of the problems which had resulted in Errington's dismissal, the difficulties with the synod and his reliance on Manning, Wiseman was more and more isolated. However, his old friends, though some of them had been very distressed by his authoritarian behaviour, did not shun him. He, too, was not unforgiving and he was prepared to be tolerant — once he had had his way — and to realise that people could differ without having to part company for ever.

In the spring of 1862 Wiseman went to Rome to participate in a canonization ceremony — precisely the sort of occasion he vastly enjoyed. Once again Rome was filled with clerics and pilgrims and there were many celebrations. In a buoyant mood he had agreed to accept the kiss of peace from his fellow English bishops; the synodical differences were officially at an end. Pius IX was delighted, and while Wiseman had in fact not really won any concessions, everyone behaved with much discretion and harmony ensued. Although indeed he did not know it, this was to be his final visit to the papal capital and it was perhaps fitting that it should be so happy an occasion.

Wiseman left Rome in June and went on to Paris where he once again was received by Napoleon III. Pius IX hoped that the cardinal might be able to persuade the Emperor to defend the papal states. The meeting was cordial enough, and the two old friends conversed amicably; but the Emperor did not commit himself. Thus, Wiseman's last mission failed, but despite his lack of success in Paris he was in good spirits. Soon after his return to London he busied himself with the round of duties of his office. The harmony which had existed in Rome between himelf and his fellow-bishops did not last and the old acrimonious criticisms reappeared, but at no point did he truly feel that he was ever in the wrong. Gradually his health again began to decline and he was less and less able to get about. He was forced to take to his bed and even when his doctors pronounced him better he was severely limited in his activities.

Although he was physically somewhat incapacitated Wiseman's combatative spirit remained strong. He publicly deplored the enthusiastic reception given to Garibaldi upon the latter's visit to England in 1863, and in a pastoral letter he expressed disapproval of the national approbation of this revolutionary and proponent of irreligious and impious ideas. *The Times* reproved him for the tone of his pastoral and accused him of having unwarrantedly charged Garibaldi with atheistical beliefs. Wiseman was furious. He pointed out in a letter to the editor of the paper that he had used *The Times's* own report of Garibaldi's position as his source. For once 'The Thunderer' climbed down and Wiseman was mollified. This was to be his last public controversy, but he was still busy with his own people. After due consideration he withdrew his support of Newman's plan for a branch of the Oratory to be sited at Oxford, for English Roman Catholics were not to be encouraged to consort with Anglicans at the university. Despite these activities he was growing increasingly enfeebled and yet at no time was he willing to speculate on his successor. All he wanted was peace, and he resisted every effort to persuade him to take any course of action which might endanger the delicate situation. Rome would decide, and its decisions would be right. By November 1864 it was clear that any major activities in the future would have to be limited, but Wiseman gave no sign of accepting the fact that his time was running out. By late December 1864 even he had to recognize facts; it was clear that he had not long to live. Throughout the month of January he grew weaker. He had all of the consolations of the Church, made peace with all whom he had offended, and died on 15 February 1865 surrounded by his devoted adherents. Manning, who had been in Rome, hastened back and arrived when Wiseman was scarcely conscious; but the old man knew he was there. On his deathbed he begged all 'to cherish peace, and charity, and unity; . . . let us put aside all jealousies and let us forgive one another and love one another.'

Wiseman was buried on 23 February 1865 and, as was probably exactly right, Manning preached the sermon. The ceremony was all that it should have been for the first regnant cardinal since Pole; it was a splendid funeral with crowds of mourners: Wiseman's journey was finished.

Perhaps he was best summed up, not by Manning who was, as might be expected, over-effusive, but in the obituary notice which appeared in *The Patriot*:

> Cardinal Wiseman, with all his faults — perhaps we might say, *in* his faults — was a thorough Englishman; and though he committed himself deeply to the Ultramontane doctrine and spirit, there was something in his English culture and full communion with English life, which tempered his Ultramontane zeal, and made him a very different man from the popular notion of a Papal emissary. A certain humane influence was shed over his life, not so much by his high intellectual culture or by his reputation for general learning; and which he was unwilling to risk by any acts or utterances of bigotry which would have shocked the sense of the English people. . . . [His] tastes and pursuits formed a link of connexion between the Prince of the Roman Church and free-minded and free-spoken Englishmen, which no mere narrow minded zealot could have established. . . .[39]

Wiseman brought the English Roman Catholic community out of the wilderness. He changed their simple, unsophisticated, rather parochial religion into that of a more urbane and 'catholic' faith. In public affairs he was often more enthusiastic than wise but even his harshest critics recognized his honesty. It is regretable that he was sometimes a poor judge of character, and that he was, there-fore, often stunned when others opposed him or impugned his motives. He supported Manning, not so much as the man, but as the agent of the Church, while his relations with Newman were never easy. This was a sad fact but true. He was a good scholar, an excellent lecturer and an able theologian. He was not particularly original in his thinking but he was able to point out the truly significant. As a man he was open, friendly and generous, vast in size, a good trencherman but no gourmet. He liked the young and they liked him, for they were able to perceive what others failed to appreciate in the Cardinal — that he had a youthful heart and a generous spirit.

His life had been successful, but the way had not been easy. Perhaps he would have been happier if he had been more cynical: but his conscience would not allow him to adopt such an attitude. Death was probably not unwelcome and he could properly feel that he had done his Christian duty in his own way. He made mistakes, was often unfair, hasty or idle; but these were only venial sins. His overall efforts had been to serve God and his Church, and both had received his full devotion.

2

On Theological Questions

Nicholas Wiseman's theological writings fall into two quite distinct categories, the first of which is homiletic in nature, designed for the edification of the members of his own communion. Such writings, including certain lectures which, incidentally, were also attended by persons other than Roman Catholics, are traditional in theology and interpretation. They are not, perhaps, as sophisticated as the writings of continental contemporaries; of course, the English Roman Catholic community of the mid-nineteenth century was somewhat insular and for a long time had not been very concerned with the intellectual aspects of their faith. Generally, however, these homiletic essays are of less significance than his other theological writings which were more directly the result of works written by Anglicans, and were formal replies to positions and ideas put forward by members of the Church of England.

It must always be remembered that Wiseman returned to England after living for a number of years in Rome. As a consequence, his personal sympathies were ultramontanist; moreover, with the advent of the Oxford Movement he expected that there might possibly be some sort of mass conversion of the Anglican communion. But it should also be remembered that Wiseman's optimism sometimes coloured his judgements, and that his views and anticipations were not generally supported by other Roman Catholics in the country.

Unlike many Roman Catholic scholars he took the Anglican theologians seriously. He never dismissed them for being unenlightened but rather he sought to demonstrate that their way led inexorably into a *cul-de-sac*. As a humane Christian he always wanted to provide them with an alternative, but he recognized, of course, that the alternative he proposed would require their formal submission to Rome. He wanted to make the movement towards Rome as easy as possible for them, and his 'Anglican' writings, in a sense, do just that. While he never fails to show the Anglican fallacies, he always endeavours to note throughout how 'Catholic' the Anglican authors actually were in their ideas or how 'Catholic' they were becoming. In other words, he makes great efforts to illustrate both the similarities and the differences between the two positions — illustrating that this was a case of 'how near but yet

48

how far.' The best of his 'Anglican' writings appeared in the *Dublin Review* at the height of the influence of the Oxford Movement, but with the conversion of Newman and his friends to Rome, this phase of Wiseman's writings comes to a close. To be sure, he did comment on other Church questions such as the Gorham case, but this was a sort of coda to his earlier contributions to the world of theological controversy.

In the preface to the third volume of his *Essays on Various Subjects*, which were a series of reprinted essays and reviews, Wiseman formulates the basis of his arguments. He had been asked frequently, 'Were the Puseyites sincere?' Very frequently in the past the Anglican Church, or some members of it at least, had appeared to have a theological outlook which was not too different from that held by the Roman Catholic communion, and it had been felt that a natural consequence of this might well have been reunion. Wiseman saw his task simply, feeling obliged 'to rescue the brands from the burning,' and to gather about him 'a saved remnant.' He observed: 'Whoever, therefore, wished to be truly their best friend, had to make up his mind to appear their most unrelenting opponent.'[1]

From the start, Wiseman was well aware that his Anglican opponents were all able men. Moreover, the ideas and theology that gradually developed following the famous sermon 'On National Apostosy' were not reiterations of previously held positions, and on no account could they be considered as Laudianism or Socinianism writ new. Rather, the new High Church Party had devised an original *schema* which to many was consistent within itself. In order to dispel the 'unreality' of such a system, 'Reasoning had to be met by reasoning; a mistaken, but a truer, reading of antiquity,'.[2] Wiseman saw himself as the guide, the parent, stern but tender, for as he so aptly put it, he hoped that '. . . during the years of affectionate opposition . . . I can say that I was never unhopeful or unloving. . . .'[3]

Because of his own view of his rôle, it was fitting that the initial number of the *Dublin Review* contained an article on aspects of the Anglican communion. Wiseman was enough of a polemicist and an Irishman to enjoy a good argument and he proceeded to comment on what was to be known as 'the Hampden Controversy.' In a few words this can be explained. On the nomination of Lord Melbourne, R. D. Hampden was appointed by King William IV to the Regius Professorship of Divinity in Oxford University. Lord David Cecil, in his biography of Melbourne, gives an engaging account of the Prime Minister receiving Hampden and calming the agitated cleric by saying, 'Be easy, I like an easy man.'[4] Prior to making the appointment, Melbourne, who, despite his outward frivolity, was much interested in theology, had consulted the Archbishop of Canterbury and had read Hampden's books. (Does any modern Prime Minister do the same today before recommending a candidate for a Regius Professorship in either Oxford or Cambridge?) Neither Melbourne nor the Archbishop found anything heterodox in Hampden's writings, but his future colleagues at Oxford, on the contrary, did.

In some of his early writings, Hampden was presumed to have expressed very unsound opinions on the Trinity and the Sacrament, but in his inaugural lecture, published early in 1836, he appeared to profess the most proper of Anglican views. Had he just changed his coat to satisfy his opponents and to keep his post, as his critics implied? Although opponents were unable to accept the sincerity of his recently enunciated lecture, they were careful to say that they had no doubts as to his fundamental Christianity; as Wiseman put it, they saw in Hampden an 'inward orthodoxy . . . [with] an outward teaching . . . in direct opposition to the principles of faith which he had professed, and to the articles of religion which he was solemnly subscribed.'[5] Wiseman disagreed and took the position that because of the peculiarities of Anglicanism, Hampden could hold whatever views he liked privately: publicly, however, he must conform to the orthodox position.

Wiseman's interpretation was very simple and he based it upon the whole history of the Anglican Church and what he believed to be its basic inconsistency. One influential element had argued that the Church had made judgments and had disapproved of heretical opinions. This group took the position that the Anglican Church had the right to condemn heresy, to censure heretics, to give judgments as the Holy Catholic Church, to say that historical interpretations coming from antiquity were not subject to private judgment and that nothing new could be added to scripture. As Wiseman did not hesitate to demonstrate, those Anglicans taking this position in their attack on Hampden were in fact denying one fundamental reason for the break with Rome since the latter always had such views which the Protestant tradition had not accepted.

According to Wiseman, the inevitable results of conflict between branches of the Anglican Church led one party to Socinianism and the other to Catholicism. In other words, Hampden's enemies had 'unguardedly, perhaps unknowingly, rejected the principles of the Reformation, and returned to thoughts and feelings which belong to other times, or at least to another Church.'[6]

Assuming for the moment that the Church of England did have

powers on matters of faith, who in fact possessed the power to take action? The Roman Catholic Church could censure Hampden through Rome if he had been a member of that Church, but did any person or persons in England have the same authority? If censure were passed, was it to be done by convocation, by the universities or by the bishops, and if done how was it to be put into effect? Those Anglicans holding opinions antithetical to Hampden's published statements might criticize him personally, but could their Church by its nature decide explicitly on such matters? On the other hand, the Roman Catholic Church could condemn the heterodox without difficulty. The Church of England claimed authority in matters of faith but could not prove it, and to Wiseman if one sincerely believed in Church authority one had to become a Catholic. The opponents of Hampden applied Catholic rationality but in an alien setting.

Wiseman took the stand that Hampden's critics were acting out of harmony with the actual situation. True, they were acting within a Catholic frame of reference but the Church of England was not Catholic, but Protestant and Hampden was a Protestant. Wiseman also asked that the High Church Party be consistent; if it wished to have Catholic ideas, it could not belong to a Protestant body. Though chiding the High Church Anglicans for maintaining their paradoxical position, but he chided them gently. He made it clear that one who supported the High Church Party, having copied Athanasius and called down 'thunder, when heresy assails her [the Church] after having satisfied himself that the Bible never was the rule of faith, but the Church its teacher . . .',[7] now discovered that such is not the case after the Reformation. Wiseman asked only that these people but consider further and carry out their ideas to the logical conclusions. If they did so they would move inevitably towards Rome and ultimately join that body. Here their 'dreams of theory . . . [would become] a reality which would satisfy their warmest longings, and fill up the measure of their just desires.' [8] Unless they were consistent in idea and action they were doomed to unhappiness, for they could only fulminate against men such as Hampden — and note that Wiseman did not — but without success. They could not have the independence of Protestantism and, at the same time, the authority of a truly 'Catholic' Church. Either they accepted a church which was able to define what was the true faith, or they would remain frustrated in a body which did not really have such power.

In essence, Wiseman was already putting forth his thesis by indicating to the members of the Oxford Movement that they could find peace in the Roman Catholic Church if they would but

51

enter it. He had demonstrated that the High Church Party simply could not attack Hampden upon the grounds it used. Powers and sanctions that were non-existentent could not be created and given a theoretical antique and orthodox base. He did not give the High Church Party any alternatives; either its members were in the Protestant tradition, that which they had to recognize and accept, or they should become Catholic and with this obtain the rights of the Catholic Church. He held firmly to the view that the Puseyites and others in the Church of England could not criticize Hampden since they and he were within the common traditions of the Anglican Church.

Having established his position, Wiseman was prepared to see what resulted. He did not write any articles on individual items which appeared in the general series *Tracts for the Times*, but awaited publication in book form. However, he read each of the *Tracts* as they appeared, and followed the general direction of the authors. To be sure, he did review *Tract #90* as an entity in itself but he considered it in conjunction with several other similar theological writings, and in any case *Tract #90* was very special indeed.

The first of his articles on the *Tracts* appeared in the *Dublin Review* in April 1838. Wiseman began by praising the *Tracts* and their authors, not because they would restore Anglicanism to a purer, more historical form but rather because the *Tracts* would expose the Church of England for what it actually was. Earlier in its attack on Hampden, the High Church Party had contended that the Anglican Church had certain powers — certainly not essentially Protestant powers — to determine what was the faith, and that these powers were based on Church councils and the historical tradition. The Protestant lays his stress on the Bible, the true Catholic on the scripture and antiquity, that is, the apostolical succession from the ancient times. But discipline had vanished in the Anglican Church because of its adherence to the Reformation. With the disappearance of discipline and authority, the powers of the episcopal body were lost. True faith could no longer be defined by any person with real authority. Wiseman asserted that the Anglican Church, by returning to what it thought or called 'primitive Christianity', had lost all contact with real Christianity.

If this were not enough, the Church of England, and in particular the High Churchmen, although claiming to return to primitive Christianity, did not do so. The obvious sign of this was not merely the service in the vernacular, but the deliberate alteration of the order of the services. The scripture commands that the Lord be praised seven times a day; the primitive church and the Roman

52

Catholic Church both followed this admonition. It is true that some corruptions had crept in during the centuries prior to the Reformation, but were these valid grounds to rewrite the order of service? Wiseman denied this firmly, reasoning that if one wished a return to primitive Christianity one would have restored the liturgy and all of its services rather than abbreviate them, thereby violating scriptural command. On the other hand, Wiseman noted that Rome corrected abuses — it did not abolish but restored — and concluded, 'Which, then, is the true lover, follower or restorer of early Christian observances?' [9]

On the question of the orders of service, it was quite correct that the Roman Catholics had preserved them — not appreciating them, so said certain Anglicans — but if Rome had not acted as a custodian of such ceremonies they would have been lost. Wiseman was charitable to the Anglicans, for he willingly assented to their assumption of any form of service — the breviary for example — which had apostolic sanction, and if properly used, could only do good. Such charity was slightly patronizing (although not so meant), for it implied that any form of service with apostolic sanction was rather better than *The Book of Common Prayer*.

Wiseman categorically denied that the Anglicans could make any claims for being a primitive church. On the other hand, considering the essentials in the early church, the Roman Catholic Church did follow the requirements laid down in antiquity and, in so doing, gave the lie to the absurd claim that the Church of England was closer to the original and primitive church. A specific example could be seen in the question of the Holy Eucharist. Prior to the Reformation, daily or at least weekly celebrations were required, but this essential element of early Christendom had vanished in the Anglican Church; but it had not vanished in the Roman Catholic communion.

Moreover, Wiseman argued that the service of the Mass had apostolic authority. The early liturgies—Roman, Egyptian, Oriental and Mozarabic — are common in many respects, but does the service of the Lord's Supper conform to such traditions? Wiseman readily showed that the reformers had 'no scruple of abolishing or completely disfiguring them.' [10] Yet the High Church Party, in what was essentially a Protestant body, admitted that the ancient liturgies ought to be venerated, and possibly re-instituted, because of their historic nature.

In other words, the Anglican Church while purporting to have been a return to a purer primitive church, a body with direct antecedents to the past, was really very novel indeed. However, many aspects of the Roman Catholic tradition which appeared

53

unique to that body were in fact not merely possessions of one communion only, but of all who were truly part of the real apostolic and historical church; and the Church of England was not part of that tradition.

He then posed the question, what had been the result of the so-called Reformation which claimed to be a return to primitive Christianity? In fact, nothing very much; indeed, Church authority, the position of the hierarchy, the basis for faith and morals, the sacraments and indeed all the great moral precepts were probably less historical than they had been in the sixteenth century. Instead of destroying the past the Roman Catholic Church retained antiquity and reformed the current practice. As Wiseman put it, 'Ours was a *conservative reform*; we pruned away the decayed part; we placed the vessel in the furnace, and, the dross being melted off, we drew it out bright and pure. Yours was *radical* to the extreme; you tore up entire plants by the roots, because you said there was a blight on some one branch; you threw the whole vessel into the fire, and made merry at its blaze. Now that you go to look for it again, you find nothing but ashes. And you are surprised at this?' [11]

The Anglican Church was not a primitive church, instead 'she fell heavily on the ground, scorched in plumage and shorn of wing, and condemned to walk or creep upon the earth's surface, and to seek her food, with dimmed eye, in its stagnant lifeless pools.' [12] The Roman Catholic Church remained directly what it had always been, while the Church of England threw away much of the apostolic tradition and rejected many ancient practices. For example, St. Gregory, one of the Church Fathers, decreed that the Mass should be performed thrice daily; but instead of following his precepts, the Anglicans created new services. In sum, Wiseman wanted to illustrate beyond contradiction that the writers of the *Tracts* could not claim to be members of a body emulating the principles of the primitive church. If he were able to be convincing then he had undermined many of the claims of the High Church Party, including its claim to true Catholicity, and thereby had diminished its fundamental theology.

In all of their statements, the Anglicans had long claimed to be part of the apostolic tradition; a claim the High Church Party insisted was not only historical but also based on adherence to a principal canon of faith, that is, the Nicene Creed. Inherent in this was the whole question of the validity of Anglican orders. Wiseman did not choose to consider the question, for he did not really think it significant. Indeed, he said quite bluntly 'that, independent of all historical questions, they [Anglican orders] are decidedly invalid and nothing worth.' He refused to take up this problem because

54

the question had been argued excessively, he allowed that even if Anglican orders were granted to be valid, the Church of England's clergy still had no rights coming with such an assumption since they could not claim to be really part of the apostolical succession because they 'are a schismatical Church in the fullest sense of the word; so that the works of their ministry are wholly unprofitable, and their jurisdiction none.' [13]

Such a statement is most severe; but Wiseman was prepared to support his arguments. He asked several questions: 'First, does consecration, even though valid, confer jurisdication? Secondly, what will vitiate the episcopacy of a see or province, or kingdom, so as to cut it off from all participation in the rights of apostolical succession and jurisdiction?' [14] It was his own response to these queries which provided the basis for his earlier strictures. Wiseman proceeded to give various examples of bishops who were validly consecrated yet had no rights to ordain or to exercise any special episcopal functions. Indeed, the Council of Nicea had taken special cognizance of the problem when it dealt with those bishops who had been consecrated prior to the decision that Donatism was heretical. Moreover, it was only the true Catholic bishop who had power; a man merely designated as a bishop did not, even though validly consecrated, automatically have the rights of government.

Anglicans, (particularly those writers who composed the *Tracts*), seemed to be confusing valid consecration with the rights of episcopal officers. Wiseman contended that, even presuming Parker and his colleagues were validly consecrated, they were not in *plenitudo potestas*. Indeed, he argued that the Elizabethan episcopate was very similar to the situation of the Donatists. These consecrations were valid, but the incumbents could only assume to be instituted by their own orthodox episcopal officer, the Patriarch of Alexandria. The Anglicans could only be instituted by the Pope, for a bishop only takes possession of his see if he does so within the canons of his Church. 'If anyone shall have been made bishop without the consent of his metropolitan, the general council defines that he ought to be no bishop.' [15] This was one of the most significant of the canons of the Council of Nicea and it was to be reiterated on a number of occasions by later Popes.

The Donatist bishops were not deposed merely by the canon of the Council of Nicea. They did not have the proper apostolical succession because they never had any jurisdiction. The Anglican response to this argument had to be made, for without it their own bishops had no jurisdiction. They had to decide whether the decisions made at Nicea were the rules for all time or whether they only applied in a specific instance. The Anglicans took the latter position and they supported a decision of the Council of Ephesus which allowed local autonomy to individual provinces. To strengthen their contention, the Anglicans took the view that the decrees of Ephesus were for ever, while those of Nicea were only applicable in a specific case. Moreover, Nicea had declared against translation of bishops from one see to another yet the Church of England practised this frequently; but at the same time the Anglicans made a case that the Church was 'governed by *fixed laws*',[16] yet acted against this philosophical position.

In summary, Wiseman's attitude on all of these questions was as follows:

> First, the Church has from the beginning, held that a bishop, however validly consecrated, if placed in possession of a see contrary to the canons actually in force in the Church, or by means contrary to those regulations which it considers essential to legitimate nomination, acquired no jurisdiction in or over it, and did not enjoy a part in that apostolical succession, which can only be transmitted through legitimate occupation. Secondly, that the canons appointing the forms of such legitimate occupation, or the bars thereto, were not particularly those of Nicea, but generally such as the Church ageed in, at a given time. Thirdly, that patriarchal jurisdiction is legitimated and determined by usage, and that this sanctions it with a force equal to the canons.[17]

Having established his position, he proceeded to call the Anglicans to account. He noted that up to 1534, Henry VIII and England accepted the authority of Rome as the patriarchal see. This was changed by Henry's legislation when he himself began appointing the bishops, a policy continued by Edward VI. Mary used the same power conferred on her by Act of Parliament to remove bishops placed in office after 1535, but she did so by acting under the traditional authority of the papacy which had been hitherto accepted and was in accord with ecclesiastical tradition. Elizabeth, on the other hand, deposed bishops who had their offices according to canon and civil law, flouting the patriarchal authority by appointing her own candidates. Could any of the Elizabethan bishops and their successors assume apostolical authority since they had usurped the position of properly validated bishops? Any court of law faced with such evidence would inevitably decide that by all precedents and customs, the Anglican hierarchy was made up of illegitimate usurpers. The Anglicans had always argued that Elizabeth's action was a restoration not a usurpation, but on what authority? They were 'named contrary to apostolical tradition, ordained contrary to the canons of the Church, nominees of the palace, thrust into sees of bishops just imprisoned and deposed by the arm of the secular power, and willing to receive episcopacy as thought it had been a mere civil dignity.' [18] Moreover, to argue that Mary's episcopate were usurpers did not mean that Elizabeth's were legitimate. Thus, according to the evidence put forward by Wiseman, by no sort of argument could the Church of England claim legitimate apostolical succession.

Having disposed of this problem, he next proceeded to consider the whole question of the schismatic and ultimately heretical state of Anglicanism. Wiseman implied that he regretted having to make such categorical statements on any religious body. To him the Anglican Church had put itself into 'The State of Schism . . . at the Reformation, and which at once acted as a blight upon all its ecclesiastical powers, withering them and rendering them incapable of any act of valid jurisdiction, or any place in the apostolical succession.' [19] By tradition a schismatic church lost all rights and could not perform any valid functions; it may be the same in belief, but unless it be part of the whole Catholic Church it could not be a true church at all.

Wiseman went further and declared that the Church of England was not only schismatical but heretical as well. On this point he cited St. Jerome who said that schism always formulates heresy to support its schismatic position or, as St. Augustine said, *'cum schismaticus sic sacrilega discussione, et haereticus sacrilego dogmate.'* [20] Wiseman also stated that the Greek Church was heretical for the same reason. At least the Anglicans were not alone in this disagreeable situation. Moreover, any church which rejected the decisions of an ecumenical council — and according to Roman Catholic doctrine both the Orthodox and Anglican Churches had done so — became heretical automatically.

The Anglicans had always made much of their essentially 'Catholic' position and had used the Church Fathers to support their claim. Wiseman used the same reasoning but came out with a contrary interpretation. He based his arguments on the Donatist Church in Africa. The story of the Donatist schism is easy to summarize. Some seventy African bishops accepted Majorinus, the predecessor of Donatus, as the true bishop of Carthage. Majorinus had been intruded into the see while Caecilianus was still in possession. The seventy presumed Caecilianus to be schismatical because of problems of his consecration. To substantiate their position a council met in Carthage under the presidency of the Bishop of Numidia, and this council decided to withdraw recognition from Caecilianus; it reported its decision to other churches in Africa. A large number of churches accepted the provisions of the council while others did not, and a schism occurred which took the name from Donatus, who became a leader.

To add to the complication, some Donatists apparently required re-baptism for their followers. However, all did not make such a demand; Donatus may have had some faulty ideas on the Trinity but most of his followers did not share his views and they accepted the traditional canons of the Church. They believed quite sincerely that they were part of the one true Catholic Church and that it was their enemies who were not Catholic. In order to resolve the question, another council was summoned in 441 to settle the matter, with St. Augustine representing the orthodox party.

The whole question really turned, not on whether one is a Christian in the most general sense, but rather whether a church is a true institution unless it is properly in communion with the whole Christian world. The premise assumed by the orthodox party, (and Wiseman took the same position), was that no national church in any circumstances was really the true church since it was not universal; that is, if a church were not in communion with many churches in all countries, then it was not the Catholic Church.

With this in mind, what was the status of the Anglican Church? It made claims to be *the* apostolic church, but the whole idea of *the* apostolic church was denied by the idea that *no* national church could make such a claim. Moreover, 'The Church of Christ' was *not* 'an aggregate of many churches, holding indeed different opinions and practices, and not actively communicating together, . . .' [21] but rather one church with all parts in communion. A schismatic church claims it has separated from some other body because the latter is corrupt — such was the argument of the reformers in the sixteenth century — but if the church were corrupt, then Christ's promise of perpetuity had failed — something the Roman Catholic Church would never accept. True, reforms were often necessary, but the body as a whole was never so corrupt as to fail totally as a body.

The Anglicans had accepted Rome as the true Church in the middle ages, but they felt it had lost this position at the Council of Trent. This interpretation was essentially a unilateral one and not necessarily accepted by other churches at all. The Anglicans have always stated they were not separatists but rather that it was Rome that had separated from the 'apostolic' and universal church. This was the Donatist argument, but as St. Augustine put it aptly, 'How can we be separatists whose communion is diffused over the entire world?' [22] Moreover, the usual development is that one schism leads to further schisms within the new independent church. The Donatists had this problem and so did the Anglicans. The main Catholic Church never had this difficulty; it was always one, and in its own opinion, remained one.

The Anglicans could send letters telling other churches that they were in communion with them but this action *solus* would not necessarily result in more than a vague reply, with no positive action occurring. A Roman Catholic bishop with letters of credence from his own primate was in communion with all other Roman Catholics. Moreover, by tradition the Bishop of Rome was the first of the bishops and, unless a church was in communion with its head, it could not be truly Catholic. Any attempt to set up another primate was automatically schismatic.

The Church fathers, and St. Augustine in particular, determined catholicity in the following fashion: 'Whether or no these persons were held in communion by the rest of the Church, that is by the aggregate of churches dispersed over the world; and *secondly*, whether they adhere to the Apostolic Roman see; . . . wherever they existed not, there was schism, and they were to have no part with those that formed it.' [23]

The Anglicans had formally renounced all dependence on Rome in 1534 and ceased communion with it. As a consequence, the Anglican Church was no longer part of the greater Catholic world, even if there had not been any doctrinal differences. The Anglicans, like the Donatists, were automatically in schism and as such had no claims to apostolical succession. In sum, Augustine's basic query remained the same: unless you are in communion with the Church Universal how can you claim to be Catholic? By reasserting the Augustinian position, the official — and to him the only logical — view of the Church, Wiseman believed that he made it clear that the position taken by the High Church Party was false; as it claimed to be based upon history, it was an example of the false use of historical facts. It appears from other sources that John Henry Newman was apparently much distressed by all these arguments for he felt that Wiseman's interpretation, solidly based as it was, destroyed many of his own contentions and those put forward by his supporters in affirming the apostolic nature of the Church of England. The appeals to history and to the concepts of the primitive church as argued in the Tracts, did not survive under such examination.

Newman's *Tract 90*, and some of the replies to it, became the basis for a later piece on the Anglican Church. In his essay, Wiseman commended Newman's article in which he had declared that acceptance of the Thirty-nine Articles was not incompatible with Roman Catholic doctrine. He further said that the Thirty-nine

Articles were drawn up before the Council of Trent where a new and official formulation of Roman Catholic doctrine had been defined, and that the Articles only opposed 'certain abuses prevalent in the Church, which the council itself in part condemned.' [24]

To Wiseman this view indicated a real development in Newman's thinking, for the latter apparently recognized that since the Church of England was not in communion with much of Christianity, it would require intercommunion to support its pretensions to universality. It might gain by establishing a contact with the Eastern churches, but essentially it required communion with Rome. Moreover, Newman had seen that not all virtue was possessed by any one body and he was willing to attempt to bend accepted Anglican doctrine to bring it more into harmony with Roman Catholicism. Previously the Anglicans had argued that Rome must rejoin Canterbury and not vice versa.

It was clear that Newman and his friends were deviating from the traditional Anglican position but in so doing, they were in a distinct minority. The mass of the Anglican Church did not regard itself as 'Catholic' in the Roman sense but rather as strictly Protestant. Wiseman thought that ultimately Newman's opinion would be universally accepted, but such was not the case at the time Newman was writing; the result was that the High Church Party could only be part of the Catholic and Apostolic Church if it made submission to Rome. Newman's critics within the Church of England recognized that Wiseman had drawn the correct implication. To preserve true Anglicanism, Newman had to be silenced, and his Oxford contemporaries attempted to do this before the whole frail fabric of Anglican precepts was dramatically destroyed.

Wiseman could afford to wait. It was clear to many that his replies to the Tracterians were skilfully argued. He consistently maintained the same high intellectual tone as they did, and never did he indulge in unnecessary polemic. He realized that his readers in the opposite camp took heed of his commentary in their own conversations and in preparing their responses.

Following the uproar over *Tract #90*, a temporary peace or, at least a silence, followed. Newman and his cohorts retired to Littlemore and the protestant faction held sway in Oxford. Wiseman knew that this was now the time for him to cease his attack. He had the High Church Party in a cleft stick; either it followed its own arguments to the logical conclusion and joined Rome or it ceased to operate on the grounds which formed the basis for its theology, that is, the appeal to the traditions of the primitive church.

In the next half dozen years, only a few articles on the subject were written by Wiseman. He very soon realized that he had made his case and that he must bide his time. In an article on 'The Anglican System' he reiterated his arguments that the idea of an Anglican branch of the Catholic Church was suppositious and impossible. There was one true Church, and the Anglican interpretation of it simply defied the scripture of antiquity. As he aptly observed, *'solis multi radii, sed lumen unum; et rami arboris multi, sed robur unum, tenaci radice fundatum. Ab arbore frenge romum germinare non poterit.'* [25]

He firmly denied the assumption that Christ is the Church and maintained that to believe so is to be misinformed. To be sure, Christ is the root from which it all comes, but Christian churches are not like branches of scientific knowledge. There is no national church. The Church of Christ alone is the repository of His promises and it totally encompasses all parts of the church. 'Our first duty is to the *Universal* Church; our second, to the Particular one. The term national we abhor when applied to His institution who knows no difference between Greek and barbarian.' [26] The stem alone is significant.

He stated further that the idea that the See of Canterbury was grafted onto Rome at the time of St. Augustine of Canterbury was nonsense. Its signficance was that Rome recognized it as a body and appointed its officers; mere apostolic succession did not make an apostolic church. It was communion with apostolic churches that made it an apostolic see, and the Anglicans simply could not claim this as arising from history. Rome was the key and remained so.

The true Catholic's position was clear. 'If we can have allegiance *either* to Rome or Canterbury, to the mother or the daughter, to the trunk or the offshoot, to the apostolic, or to the episcopal, see, we yield it willingly, lovingly and irrevocably to the former. Let Canterbury do its duty; let it seek and obtain communion from the chair of St. Peter, and from the great body of bishops throughout the world, and we will bow ourselves before the primatial chair, lower than the lowest, and reverently kiss the jewelled hand of its occupier, and promise him all canonical obedience; but so long as he and his suffragans are not recognized by the Church Catholic, as an actual living, communicating portion thereof, we recognize and know them not, we have no part in them or with them. . . .' [27]

Wiseman claimed that the Anglican Church, which placed so much emphasis on its historic nature, in fact had no feeling for history. The liturgy was maimed, the sacraments were reduced and the Anglican Church was a truncated and ruined object. To regain her beauty was not a difficult process, but Anglicans must not pretend that they were beautiful.

Despite all contention to the contrary, the Anglicans were Protestants; they had no right to claim the title Catholic, and their hierarchy had no special authority. Anglicanism was not homogenous; Catholicism was. Above all, who represented the Anglican Church? The Archbishop of Canterbury, parliament or the sovereign?

There is little doubt that Wiseman was very influential in demonstrating to those of the High Church Party the view that if they followed the logical conclusion of their ideas, their only true road led inexorably to Rome. Some, like Newman and his circle at Littlemore, became Roman Catholics, while others remained 'invincibly ignorant' and failed to accept Wiseman's arguments; they saw much truth in what he said, but not the final truth. As a result, men like Keble and Pusey remained in the Church of England. But, the immediate effect of Wiseman's arguments was that the Anglican Church as a whole was forced to reconsider its dogmatic approach. To be sure, the protestant element did not disappear, far from it, but more and more writings appeared which attempted to demonstrate that Rome and Canterbury had much in common. Wiseman's view was that this was an unreality, for he was naturally and unalterably opposed to attempts to utilize certain 'Catholic' symbols which really had no meaning for 'real' Anglicans. He thought Anglicans were 'unreal' in trying to stretch the words of the communion service into being in harmony with Roman Catholic beliefs. It was impossible for 'real' Anglicans to accept transubstantiation; but by playing with words, different terms could *seem* to mean the same thing; but seeming is not actuality. Moreover, by 'the church' the Anglican meant the Church of England to the exclusion of all others while the Roman Catholic had the view that 'One Church' was a union of all churches in communion with Rome. 'The Church is one, by perfect unity in doctrine, by communion, by common headship, and indivisible government. All out of union with its centre are excluded from our belief. We believed that she teaches, and know how she teaches it. She is an infallible guide; and whoever refuses her obedience is cut off from her, and must perish if he repent not.' [28]

By 1847 the Oxford Movement was a spent force. The Tractarians had been dispersed, but the High Church position still existed. Wiseman found another opportunity to comment on the High Church group when he reviewed Keble's volume *Sermons, Academical and Occasional*. In this book Keble, as one who had not accepted Wiseman's position and had not followed Newman to Rome, was trying to resolve all the doubts of 'the saved remnant.' His aim was to prevent conversion. He argued that the Anglican Church was 'the safer way', begging his fellow Anglicans to remain in the Church of England because it was proper to stay where God initially placed them. Since there was 'generous contentment in such a state,' they were to 'remain because of intellectual modesty if only because it is easier and simpler, remain because of the dangers of religious intellectual controversy which only leads to distress and unhappiness.' [29] Keble felt that the Church of England was comprehensive enough to include a wide spectrum of belief: it was easy for the Anglican to accept the Godly man in all churches, while the Roman Catholic could accept his own. It was better even to live with doubts, he had asserted, than to leave one's church and so bring upon one all the inevitable, resulting complications.

Keble's arguments only proved to Wiseman how weak the Anglican position actually was; but what could one expect of a church created by law? Later he was to make much of this idea in his scornful analysis of the Gorham judgment which to him showed inexorably that the Church of England was not only protestant but erastian as well. Wiseman had not patience with Keble's plea that his fellow Anglicans continue to accept an illogical and unhistorical set of premises. Wiseman was somewhat ironical in noting that Hampden, once the object of criticism, and now named to the episcopal bench by Lord John Russell, was not attacked by Keble on the grounds of *quieta non movere*.

Wiseman's essays on the Anglican Church may be said to conclude with a final one on 'the Gorham Case'. In this article he reiterates anew the thoroughly anamolous position of the Anglican Church. He was aware that many Anglicans were distressed by the decision of the courts, and he knew that some proposed a sort of new non-juring church. He responded to this idea by quoting a member of the High Church Party — apparently this individual later became a Roman Catholic — as saying 'No, no; we have already got out of the ship into the boat, let us not think of getting out of the boat into the tub.' [30]

In all his numerous writings on the Anglican Church, Wiseman never failed to state that he respected those who belonged to it; he had no doubts as to their sincerity, but to him they were on a losing wicket. Their appeals to antiquity in support of their claims to be a Catholic and apostolic church he felt he had refuted, and his argument that the Anglicans were simply the new Donatists had a great effect. Those who strained after Roman Catholic doctrines and practices he knew were not advancing their cause, for they could not truly believe in such doctrines and remain in the Church

63

of England, and if they did remain Anglicans they were certainly not honest.

In an essay on the writings of Hurrell Froude he summed up all of his views on those Anglicans who truly sought to find the faith. He hoped all were in this category.

> Peace be to him! [and to all good Christians] is our parting salutation. The hope which an Ambrose expressed for a Valentinian, who died yet a Catachumen, we willingly hold of him. His ardent desires were with the truth; his heart was not a stranger to its love. He was one, we firmly believe, whom no sordid views, nor fear of men's tongues, would have deterred from avowing his full convictions, and embracing their consequences, had time and opportunity been vouchsafed him for a longer and closer search. He is another instance of that same mysterious Providence, which guided a Grotious and a Leibnitz to the threshold of truth, but allowed them not the time to step within it, into the hallowed precincts of God's visible Church.[31]

Some of his Protestant 'friends' did find 'the time'; others, of course, did not: but Wiseman remembered them all in his prayers, and recognizing that they were 'beloved enemies' or 'beloved friends'; and each and every one was a recipient of his love and charity.

If Wiseman's theological writings in response to the whole tractarian movement were his best, what of the many other articles, essays and lectures that were published? These were largely more popular in nature and were designed for the widest of audiences, both clerical and lay, Roman Catholic and Protestant. He never summarized in one major work his views on the Church and its beliefs; rather he wrote for the moment, with the result that there is no coherent statement of his position.

Regretfully but truthfully it must be realized that Wiseman did not have either a very supple or a very original mind. He was limited in his understanding of subtle concepts, but at the same time he was able to talk and write about ordinary theological and religious questions in a straightforward fashion. His ideas were expressed simply — albeit he had a somewhat convoluted style — and were nearly always pedagogical in tone. He was very much at his ease as the teacher and he firmly believed that it was the duty of clerics to educate their parishioners and others as well, and to make known to the world at large the basic beliefs of the Church.

Other theological interests he had were largely linguistic in nature, as is evidenced in his first published work. His *Horae Syriacae* which appeared in 1827 was a set of three essays — with all the heavy scholarly appurtenances — of which one was a theological discussion for a professional audience, of the phrase *Hoc est einem corpus meum*. The other two sections were very specialized philological studies on Syriac versions of the *Old Testament*. Scholars were most favourably impressed by the knowledge and research evident in the *Horae Syriacae*.

Nevertheless, this early effort of Wiseman, which was really a sort of thesis and which gained him his chair, was not at all typical of his later efforts. True, it did promote his academic career in Rome, and his concern for linguistic and philological pursuits long remained a personal enthusiasm. However, with his public life becoming more and more important after the 1830's, this scholarly activity gradually lapsed or became very much of a secondary interest at best. In all his more general writings, he assumed a reasonably knowledgeable audience but not in a professional sense. To be sure, he always acted on the assumption that his audience was interested in the topic at hand. On a very few occasions he felt that he had to convince, and his remarks had to be delivered in such a way as to create an enthusiasm. Generally, he was less concerned to inspire than to elucidate.

As may be expected, Wiseman's theology was extremely orthodox. Speculative thought was not his *métier*; his beliefs were simple and were accepted without real analysis. At no time did he attempt anything like Newman's *oeuvre*. Perhaps this is why, in this century, Wiseman is largely unread; his resolutions of problems seem too simple and not particularly applicable to a more questioning generation. In matters concerning his own faith and that of his Church, he had, after a brief period of doubt as to his own fitness to become a priest, no desire to question orthodox doctrine. When and if he posed questions, they were only hypothetical ones to provide a structure for his arguments and the answers to the questions were predetermined.

In dealing with religious ideas and theological questions for members of his own communion, Wiseman did not really indulge in any discussion or real dialogue. He expounded on matters of faith but did not assume or expect to receive any adverse commentary on his remarks. Because of his training and professional career at the university, combined with his spiritual authority, he never doubted that he had a rather special position. This is not to say that he denigrated the work of other theologians in England — far from it — but he did always feel that their work could only receive final approbation when and if it had a Roman basis. To him scholarship — and this included all forms of theology — lacked the *finesse*, the *imprimatur*, without actual experience in the Roman

65

schools. Although he frequently said that he did not like controversy, he was often at his best in this field. His writings, directed towards the non-Catholic world, have a rigour and style which those composed for his own particular denomination lack. Perhaps this arose from his own innate sureness of belief, which made him assume that all others of the Catholic faith were as staunch in their convictions as he was.

Upon his return to England in 1836, Wiseman accepted an invitation to give a series of lectures on the Roman Catholic Church. These lectures were later published with the rather ponderous title *The Real Presence of the Body and Blood of our Lord Jesus Christ in the Blessed Eucharist proved from Scripture*. The occasion of these lectures, delivered to a very mixed audience of Roman Catholics and Protestants, was significant in that it was the first time in England since the Reformation that a leading Roman Catholic cleric was able to talk on a public platform about the basic beliefs of the Roman Catholic Church. Certainly, this was one of the initial consequences of Catholic emancipation and implied a wide degree of tolerance which had not existed before. As with the lectures on science and religion which he had delivered in Rome, those on Catholic doctrine were not speculative but were often couched in technical and specialized language.

Wiseman took the opportunity to state categorically what he was to say at many other times, namely, that the Roman Catholic Church was the one and only orthodox body. He denied that mere belief in the Christian teachings, however sincere, made one a member of the Church. Formal membership of the Church was essential, for without it the road to salvation was frought with danger. He never went so far as to say that those who were not members of the Roman Catholic Church were automatically damned, for he did not presume to know the inscrutable ways of God, but he did hold that salvation outside the Church was something that transcended ordinary practice.

Whenever he used the word 'Church' he did so in a very specific fashion meaning an institution or body that was in communion with the apostolic see. To Wiseman, the Church was an organic body which could assimilate a great variety of ideas. At this juncture he believed that religious thought and practice ought to be broad and conciliatory, although his views altered later in his ardent championing of the *Syllabus of Errors*. In the 1830's he was very much a 'Catholic' in the broadest sense, but he firmly rejected anything that was incompatible with the teachings of the Church as defined by the church fathers, the general councils and the papacy. He took the view that within this all-embracing framework, any essentially 'Christian' ideas could be incorporated. While accepting a 'Catholic' view he also limited it simultaneously by adopting the stance that certain canons of faith were never to be questioned. Matters of faith as defined by the Church had to be accepted; disobedience meant expulsion. Because Wiseman had an uncomplicated view of his own religious beliefs, he did not think that religious ideas should be subjected to too much rationalizing and philosophizing, for the elements of mystery in the Christian faith were so very essential to its whole nature.

As may be immediately understood, one of the most vital elements of the Christian faith was an acceptance of the doctrine concerning transubstantiation; to accept this essential element of mystery through faith was to be truly Christian. He denied absolutely that transubstantiation could be put into a coldly intellectual and rational concept; it was not subject to reason. It was on this point that the protestant thinkers and writers had erred. He was absolutely sure that this mystery was an essential bond with Christ. The Anglican Church had destroyed the mystery and by so doing was cast out from the true Church. Wiseman sympathized with those Anglicans who had attempted to preserve the mystery or to recover it as an essential in their theology, but the consequence of its rejection by the Church of England in its official capacity was that no person remaining in that communion had the same direct relationship with Christ as did the Roman Catholic.

The direct contact made by Christians with the living and risen Christ was through the eucharist which Christ had established as the essential aspect of the whole message and philosophy of the Christian religion. The eucharistic service was a repeat of the divine sacrifice made by Christ for man's salvation, and its repetition occurred each time the Mass was said. Wiseman never failed to point out that the Anglican communion service was not performed in the daily service — indeed, often it was done only a few times each year — and hence the relationship of Christ and the Church was not continually maintained. The communion service was not the eucharist and no member of the High Church Party in the Church of England could find a real means of proving it to be so. The communion service lacked the sacrificial element and, although it was not merely a memorial service in the ordinary protestant tradition, it lacked the vital nature. Only the Roman Catholic Church, with its emphasis on the eucharist as the central element in the service, maintained Christ's relation with man. The sacrifice in the Mass which was performed by the priest every day meant that the Church reaffirmed its contact with Christ and his Church from its origins.

In an article entitled 'A Letter Respectfully Addressed to the Rev. Dr. J. H. Newman' which appeared in 1841, Wiseman re-emphasized the importance of basic Catholic theology in the Christian tradition; he reaffirmed the significance of the Virgin, the doctrine of purgatory and the rôle of the saints and miracles. He wished to make certain that his own co-religionists knew precisely what were the doctrines of their own church and he also wished to ensure that the Anglicans supporting the Oxford Movement could not claim essential catholicity. Any who failed to accept the fundamental doctrines of the Church as laid down by Rome were at best in the category of the Donatists in the time of Augustine.

Wiseman regarded non-Catholic views of the holy mysteries as merely scholarly, without heart. To him only a Catholic could truly appreciate the Virgin birth, the childhood of Christ, the significance of the Passion, the rôles of the saints. Only a Catholic had the necessary sensitivity and affection; the protestant mind was too rational, too cold. The Protestant always reasoned; the Catholic received the impressions which were the true manifestations of faith.

What of grace and forgiveness? He argued that they were the significant elements which arise from the knowledge of repentance from sin. In the protestant tradition they result either from a personal act or from a general absolution, both of which Wiseman would regard as mockery. The Catholic, on the other hand, makes his confession, performs the necessary penance prescribed and receives final absolution from his confessor. The priest has been given the right to confer absolution through his office and as part of that divine grace granted to him with the sacrament of ordination. The erstwhile sinner knows that he is truly one with God by participating in the Holy Eucharist. The sinner is sinner no more; he is safe in the arms of Christ, recognized once again as the son of the Father. Can any Anglican make such a claim for his Church?

Moreover, he argued, the Catholic Church alone realizes the true significance in the scriptures, particularly of the parables. For example, in the parable of the prodigal son, the father's house is the house of the Christian within the Church; the prodigal's story and his return is that of the individual's progress towards salvation. The Roman Catholic Church alone is able to convey divine forgiveness just as the father forgave the son; above all, the feast prepared for the prodigal son is the same joyful festival of the mystery of the Holy Eucharist.

According to Wiseman the whole of scripture, the teaching of the apostles and the church fathers continuing in the living church, merely serve to emphasize the rôle of the Roman Catholic Church. The entire Christian tradition summarizes the problem of man in his fallen condition and the road to his redemption. The Church's message is one of ultimate joy. As a sort of a coda to his interpretation of the scripture, Wiseman did not fail to recognize the need for a more critical study of the scriptures, for he did comprehend that the Catholic often tended to be too romantic in his view of the Bible. A proper study of the Bible could be a valuable aid in understanding and he thought that the Protestants ought not to have the monopoly on such critical studies, since the Catholic could bring his special attributes of faith to a close study of the scriptures, adding to the edification of the faithful.

The rôle of the miraculous as illustrated in the scriptures was important to Wiseman, because it was further proof of Christ's truth. The miracle, whether performed directly by Christ or by those who came after him, vindicated the claims of Christ that His teachings were of divine origin. The miracle was more than that, for it forced the attention of the public on the Christian message, and also helped to persuade the unenlightened of the truth, making them willing to accept the Christian message. Yet he also saw the miracles of Christ in yet another rôle. For example, the casting of the net by the disciples in the Sea of Galilee was the Church (united, since the net does not break) seeking the souls of men. Christ ordered his apostles to act, and they complied; he orders the Church to act and it complies in the catching of souls. Both the heavily laden nets in Galilee and the many converts in the net of the Church were results of God's action.

Miracles have the further effect of showing that God can act out of time and space which mere mortal man cannot do. That God is able to act in a non-rational fashion proves that by using his agents — Christ or the saints — His special powers transcend any self-inspired powers of man alone. Miracles as enunciated in the scriptures have other analogies with the Church in its present state. The miracle told in *Mark* Chapter VII, of the restoration of hearing and speech to the deaf and dumb man, is the basis for baptism ceremony used for adult converts. The Christian is like the man whose sight has been restored. To summarize, it is only in the Catholic Church that these miracles of the scriptures have their modern counterparts in action and belief. Thus the miraculous, in this respect, is one further manifestation of the truly apostolic nature of the Roman Church.

Of course, the miracle of miracles is the Holy Eucharist. The latter is the 'Sacrament of Love' and 'Love' is compassion — *caritas*, not *amore*. It is seen in one guise in the story of the loaves and fishes when Christ miraculously fed, through his compassion, a multitude of five thousand. Yet He did not create four or five loaves, rather He fed the people with the original five. This is the same as the bread in the Eucharist; it is not the individual consecrated wafer one eats but rather the original wafer that is Christ's body. The miracle of transubstantiation can also be seen in the scriptural account of Christ's life. At the marriage feast at Cana the water at the feast is changed into wine, the whole process of divine mutation. This is repeated but in a higher form in the Mass when the wine is changed to the blood of Christ. Moreover, it is a greater miracle since it does not occur visibly; it is accepted by faith and not through reason.

The Eucharist is Jesus Christ on earth. A Catholic gains a sense of peace by merely being in the presence of the Eucharist for he is with Christ. Moreover, this special sense cannot be felt by Protestants, for to them the communion is a totally different thing. The Catholic is compelled to fall down and worship the Eucharist and the real presence, while the Anglican seems to kneel for the wrong reason, that is to say, merely because it is commanded in the *Book of Common Prayer*, not because Christ is present.

There was no doubt in Wiseman's mind that the Catholic Church was totally consistent. Miracles may be rare, but they do occur — the power to work miracles was given to the apostles and to the saints later — and, it should be added, so do other non-rational spiritual acts of true worth. God and Christ have given grace and this is as real as nature, for there is not only a physical life but also a spiritual life. Christ is present in all of the sacraments. Man — that is, apostles, saints or priests — may perform the visible act, but Christ alone *really* performs the acts. Miracles are evidences of Christ's actions, outward and visible signs; the true Catholic believes in these miracles and does not accept the idea that the age of miracles is over.

To share in this great communion with Christ one must become a participant through baptism. Wiseman took the view that a valid baptism automatically made the individual a member of the Catholic Church. Any Christian who believed sincerely could baptise and even the Protestant had it within himself, if validly baptised, to experience Christian grace and the hope of salvation. One only lost this chance by a volitional act. The Protestant committed a very grave sin by baptising children into the Holy Catholic and Apostolic Church and then denying them the full attributes of that Church. Moreover, the Protestant seemed wilfully to deny the true significance of one of the Christian Church's greatest of miracles.

One of the questions that was still a vital issue to nineteenth-

70

century society was that concerning papal authority. When Wiseman issued his famous letter in 1850, it appeared to many of his contemporaries that he believed that Rome had all-encompassing authority with political as well as spiritual powers. The reaction of the British public generally to such a stance was most unfavourable and Wiseman hastened to correct the misapprehension concerning political authority. Wiseman's position on this question can be seen in an early article in the *Dublin Review* entitled 'The Authority of the Holy See in South America', in which he presented a coherent explanation of his general viewpoint.

In his article he begins with the basic assumption that the Pope alone can institute and confirm bishops, a power given to him at the Council of Nicea. It was held, then, that should any other than the Pope hold such power the Church would not be free and in an unfree church the secular authority would inevitably obtrude itself and control the Church. This was the consequence of the Henrician revolution. Are there limitations on papal powers such as appear in concordats? In fact, no, for although the Pope may permit secular rulers to nominate episcopal candidates, institution alone is papal. Moreover, and this should be emphasized, the right to nominate is a favour granted by Rome and is not a secular right.

Wiseman also argued that only the Pope could have the certain knowledge of the orthodoxy of the candidate to be instituted, at least at the time when the individual was named. Since orthodoxy is determined by the Pope, those who followed his beliefs were by definition orthodox. If each individual secular ruler determined orthodoxy for himself, heterodoxy would ensue, and this would be followed inevitably by schism and heresy. Critics have argued that to grant Rome such final and arbitrary authority is dangerous. Wiseman's view was that the pontiff, by being free from the taint of a national state and by being a supra-national, guaranteed that true religious freedom was ensured. By being outside any national system, the Pope was not subject to local pressures, and this prevented a situation such as existed in the case of the Church of England whose bishops were creatures of the reigning government, and whose purely secular considerations over-rode Christian concerns. The pontiff, being free of such limitations, would not be curtailed by political decisions. Besides, the Pope was responsible to God and not to the state or a parliamentary majority.

As a result, Wiseman argued, the papacy alone can protect ecclesiastical unity since the men chosen by the Pope are loyal to the Church and not to a party in the state. This gives to them a similar freedom of action; the people would know that such men are biassed only towards the preservation of the Church and its

71

traditions while, at the same time, being perceptive enough to know that political figures are loyal only to the interests of their own party. If there be a conflict of loyalties, the political viewpoint is more likely to be served. The Church is governed by God, not by man, and the Pope, as God's Vice-regent, is inspired by the Holy Spirit. The Church does not act as a secular agency for itself, but in order to promote Christian welfare all over the world; the Church acts in a universal not in a particular sense. The Church has established procedures to promote its aims, using not only the Pope but also councils and synods. Its policies are put into practice through canon law which is not immutable; changes can occur as the need arises but they are not enacted to satisfy mere expediency; they must conform to the traditions. The Church acting in the secular world is not an ossified body and canon law is constantly being refined to enhance and to promote the world of faith. The sole purpose of the Church is to act in direct harmony with God's will.

To bring men closer to the perfectibility of faith, Wiseman advocated the reading of devotional literature and he wrote a couple of volumes of meditations for ordinary laymen. His ideas in these books were not profound, but they were expressed in such a way that they were readily comprehensible. He believed in simplicity and clarity for he realized that highly sophisticated ideas would not readily appeal, and that over-complicated works would remain unread. His successor at Westminster, Herbert Vaughan, said of Wiseman's ideas and sentiments, 'if not new, . . . at least [they were] presented in a new light or reference. Thus, even where there is much that is trite and familiar, you will suddenly come upon a gem which will more than compensate for any sense of labour or defect in style.' [32]

Wiseman had very definite views on what constituted the best of devotional reading; he believed it to be found in the writings of the early Church fathers or as expressed through the liturgy which combined the beauty of faith with the sublime and holy. Because he was a conservative he felt that ideas expressed in writings that had stood the test of time had an appeal, while more modern statements were harsh and abrasive. Similarly, the traditional church architectural style and building stood for the old beliefs in a tangible form; the new was less spiritual and more garish. Wiseman personally really felt that devotional literature should consist of the more historical texts, but he knew that they were often abstruse. Consequently he felt obliged to provide other more general writings which might have been less melifluous, but did resolve the difficulties of understanding.

72

He was firm in his conviction that prayer brought man closer to the Infinite, and he constantly emphasized the importance of the prayers in the Breviary. He also took the view that since prayers composed by the saints transcended prayers by ordinary men, they should be used and read often. He rather caustically observed that many modern writers memorialized God instead of praying to Him. Partly because of his linguistic interests and partly because he left that traditional language and usage had a special quality, he was convinced that modern speech was less in harmony with the whole act of prayer than traditional speech. Here he is at one with the Roman Catholics of to-day who are opposed to the Mass in the vernacular. He felt that ancient language was more sonorous, more respectful and more inclined to turn us towards God. Holy and pious writings should express gratitude and *caritas* and fly to heaven; they should show ardour, not just duty. He likened pious writings in contemporary style to green wood which, unlike perfumed cedar, will not blaze up brilliantly and in a moment. Wiseman did not feel with the angels in hearing prayers written in the language of his own time; rather he was left somewhat bereft and often with the most mundane of feelings.

What is prayer Wiseman asked? The answer was that it is something that should be both public and private, best noted in the Mass where the priest alone really participates, but in all other services something communal. Prayer is solemn but not sanctimonious or lugubrious, for prayers are an expression of mutual love. As a result, the spirit should not only be inspired by the sentiment but should also be full of joy and happiness. Prayer should not imply weariness and a sense of obligation alone; one should have a penitential spirit certainly, but also be filled with the full knowledge in the final love of God. The Church offices performed by the devout exemplify all that Wiseman thought that the best forms of prayer should be.

What might be the ideal form of prayer? One is poetical and one merely a statement in plain language. The former is the one which is the major element of the daily formal liturgy of the Church. Poetic prayer has a form and an essential style, and in such prayers God is recognized in His greatest power. These prayers are often partly composed of scripture or from the meditations of the saints, both of which are forms of the highest poetic nature. There is a grandeur in the simplicity of language, for truly sublime poetry is so often expressed without literary embellishments. Plain chant to Wiseman was purer art than the best Italian opera. Thus, poetical prayer expresses the highest and most sublime of emotions, that is, the love of God.

Wiseman emphasized that prayer during the celebration of the Mass was not the only form of prayer, and he strongly believed that private prayer and meditation were important as well. To gain the greatest benefit from private prayer he advocated the reading of the breviary and the recitation of the rosary. By concentrating on such forms of prayer, the Christian was brought into a personal confrontation with God. The greatest of sins was the absence from God, and a failure to approach Him means that man is helpless; prayer makes the Man of Sorrows become the Lamb of God. One should be 'confused' with the Holy Spirit: the verbal prayer is but the medium for what is the essential element, namely, the carrying of the message of devotion to the Heavenly Father.

None of this is new, but it is a reaffirmation of the traditional viewpoint. Throughout all of his Catholic writings Wiseman tended to express the orthodox mode of thought of the Church. He did not attempt to put forth the unique, and he was at his best when he proceeded to re-state the historical position of his belief. He wrote for a public that was sympathetic to what he was saying, but at the same time he thought that the mass of society needed educating. He was convinced that most of the public wanted to do the right thing, but was unsure of the way. He did not write great theological works. His own mind was unsubtle, as was his faith. While he was a good scholar he was not an original thinker. He was a practical parish priest and he saw all of the English Catholic community as his parish. He was a popular writer, for he wrote with the mass audience in mind, and he did not care excessively that he was not appealing to the intellectual world. Wiseman loved all men, particularly the common man, and wrote his theology for them which may well explain most cogently why he was read widely in his own day. But conditions change, and his writings, unlike those of Newman, now seem unsophisticated and somewhat naïve.

3

Views of Art and its Practitioners

For many years it was fashionable to make perjorative remarks about nineteenth-century philistinism, but more recently the situation has changed and the Victorians are now seen in a more sympathetic light, though they are often assumed to have had no real opinions about art with their almost excessive enthusiasm for realism and for anecdotal painting. There is still a tendency to believe that Dobsonianism — that is, an attitude which expresses the view that 'I know nothing about art but I know what I like' — was the order of the day. Certainly a vast number of people did subscribe to such an opinion then, as they would now, but there were many others who had decided views on art and its rôle in man's life. Art had a function, but it was not necessarily functional.

Nicholas Wiseman was not a professional art critic — relatively few such individuals existed then — but in common with many of his contemporaries, he did not hesitate to record his opinions on art. By so doing he enabled posterity to have yet another view on what an educated, and for that time enlightened — in the best sense — individual wanted art to do.

To him the problem initially required a definition of the phrase 'perception of natural beauty.' He believed that this demanded 'the power of noting and relishing the distinctive and characteristic graces of nature in every part of creation, . . . elegance of form, . . . whatever pleases, delights, and raises the thoughts of men, in the contemplation of natural objects.' [1] Even so, he believed that merely having this attribute in itself was insignificant, since an essential requirement of the artist was the ability to communicate this perceptivity in some fashion. The artist must be able to transmit 'the impression which nature's beauties make upon our own minds and souls; . . . becoming her mirrors, not insensible ones, but endowed with a power of combining, harmonising, condensing things distant and heterogeneous, and producing pictures which no other eye has gathered together . . . and projecting them on others' minds.' [2] However, 'artistic beauty' is not the same as the 'perception of natural beauty'. Anyone may readily be able to enjoy 'natural beauty' in its original setting since this does not require any special talent. Few indeed exist who lack this ability but most are incapable of communicating this personal pleasure.

For Wiseman, the classical world, with all its great attributes, which he readily acknowledged, lacked not only the ability to perceive natural beauty but still more the facility to communicate it. The classical world had no idea of setting art within a landscape, that is to say, within the realm of natural beauty. He was certain that the reason why classical artists failed to appreciate natural beauty — although he recognized their supremacy in plastic forms — was that they lacked what he would call 'love'.

According to his definition, love required a sense of nature, an affection for it. One must not merely know nature, (the classical world knew it in an intellectual sense) but nature must be pursued with a passion. The true artist must not present an 'external view of nature', not 'a looking at it, as outside himself', but rather he must have 'an image of her [nature] in his own mind which he describes; for he identifies himself with . . . her, with such hearty love, and such delicate appreciation, as [to] prove how . . . deeply her forms were graven on his heart.'[3] The resultant work, seen with true natural perception, was 'shaped in the mind' with the original 'hidden amidst treasures of creative art, . . .'[4] However, love of nature alone was insufficient; it had to undergo certain natural and proper alterations prior to being expressed in art. The youth expressed his regard with enthusiasm, the older artist did so by refining his early sentiments and obtaining a more mature, a more noble form. Often merely voluptuous, youthful affection was not necessarily true 'love', since love must be noble, and above all moral; without these requisites, the artist could not hope to communicate what he had perceived. Love was 'pure and innocent' but at the same time 'a step to higher and better feelings.'[5] The mature artist had an enlarged means of observation that came from experience and from the understanding of love.

Love properly comprehended is explicable in Christian terms and Christian values. To quote Wiseman again, 'Nature is only the expression, God the reality. Natural beauty is stated but only in terms of a "love" that arises from a divine and hence higher source.'[6] Further, he noted that 'There appears to me something sublime in . . . nature linked, through its laws, with God and every part conscious of its connection.'[7] A 'perception of natural beauty' so understood, could not fail to create an art that expresses what beauty truly is, that is a reflection, a mirror-image of the divine work of God. At the same time human art is both creative and destructive. Spiritual action created nature; man destroys nature by using its artifacts to attempt to portray the actions of the divine. Art has a soul: 'God seen in Nature, becomes the obvious perception of its greatest beauty,'[8] and art in its highest form is

Christian. Only when it *is* Christian, does the true 'union between love of nature and deep religious spirit'[9] express its proper sentiments.

Wiseman attempted to clarify his viewpoint in a specific fashion by referring to Pietro Periegino, who, to him, painted what he called 'the marked outlines' showing 'the evening cloudless sky, with its bright amber passing through, and defining clearly the opening of the belfry [of St. Peter's in Montorio].'[10] Evidently nature supports what is really true and to see this essential truth, one must have 'love' because 'natural love rises to the supernatural; from the affections of nature [it] raise[s] us to the adoration of nature's God.'[11] Only the Christian eye can enlarge the area of contemplation, uniting 'many portions of this shattered glass [the whole of nature] . . . to give us at least a partial glimpse of that everlasting Beauty. . . .'[12]

With what he called 'perception', Wiseman also demanded a 'philosophy of art'. In classical antiquity he noted that 'the paintings of Polygnates served as a text book for the moral lessons of the philosopher Chrysippus;' and quoting Aristotle to highlight his idea of 'philosophy of art' he added that 'painting teaches the same precepts of moral conduct as philosophy, with this advantage, that it employs a shorter method.'[13] Therefore, art was to be a force for social progress; if it became merely an imitation of nature and that alone, it had no value.

He was also convinced that in the Christian tradition, art served the purpose which Aristotle ordained. The classical world had its activities 'bounded by time and space' while the Christian world, limited as it was '*in expression*, was in its *allusions* infinite.'[14] Christian art was able to draw on the known theology of man's true destiny, that is, salvation. The special nature of Christian art was further emphasized by 'the beauty and eloquence of expression . . . the vastness and importance of its compositions . . . [with] their great moral influence as one of the forms of language.'[15]

The true philosophy of art demands the essential Platonic concept of 'the idea', but the latter does not exist, in its ultimate sense, without being related to time and space. This means that to 'the idea' must be added geometrical (drawing) and harmonious (colour) aspects or elements. With these essential additions the artist as philosopher can create, and the art which results is essentially related to 'the idea'. The best — and Wiseman does not hesitate to use the superlative degree — is 'the idea' that is permeated with Christian values. Lesser forms he describes as 'Paganism', arising from classical antiquity, and 'Naturalism' seeking sources from nature alone. The best form of art he designates as the mystical school which is inspired by the soul 'vivified by the doctrines and traditions of Christianity . . .' [16] since only the mystical school embodies the essential unity of art by expressing 'the idea'. Art, once betraying its true philosophical origin and representing paganism or naturalism, was essentially decadent, for it no longer guided moral conduct.

According to Wiseman, an excellent example of the non-mystical school was Byzantine which he dismissed as 'the leprosy of art'.[17] The Byzantine artists appeared to support St. Cyril's incorrect view 'that the Redeemer, externally, was the most ignoble and abject of his race.' [18] Not only did such opinions hold in the Byzantine world, but they began to infect western art with 'the frightful conceptions of Byzantine imagination.' [19] Of course this was a complete denial of 'the idea' and obviously also of paganism and naturalism. It was only when this temporary aberration was discarded in the west that artists were able to return to proper perceptions and activities.

Art must ever be watchful of 'decay'. The mystical school is subject to the sin of naturalism; there comes to be 'an undue importance to particulars, and by confounding the sign with the thing signified, through the insidious tendency of this error, men finished by quitting the substance and pursuing the shadow.' [20] Paganism also undermines the mystical school in a very special fashion. In order to attain the highest form of 'the idea' the mystical school wanted to use the best means at hand to attain this end. It sought inspiration from the false values of the pagan school based upon rationalism rather than faith, and thereby the artist, by working through the science of perspective, came to be seduced by essentially pagan objects. The emphasis was not only on classical antiquity, but on natural objects in themselves. Thus, Christian values and especially *caritas* was lost completely, with only externals remaining.

Nevertheless, art based upon the mystical had a life of its own, independent of other forces, since the innate sentiments inspired by philosophy and expressing the internal verities managed to survive. Indeed, in some Italian artistic circles they became paramount and thereby restored the mystical school. The latter, united not only the elements — geometrical and harmonious — but also 'the idea'. Drawing and colour were the means to expression; they were not, as in decadent art, the ends alone.

Regrettably, in Wiseman's view, many artists succumbed to naturalism and paganism, with the result that art no longer purified and exalted the soul, no longer raised it 'above the ephemeral conditions of time and space, into the eternal regions of real being.' [21] The artist abandoned his duty to inculcate moral conduct

78

and lost the view of the beatific vision. The artist entertained, but he did not inspire because he had lost his vitality and was only an imitator of the natural world, perceiving beauty only externally. The living model may be the base, but the artist must see from within.

Only a few of Wiseman's contemporaries attempted to recapture this lost vitality. He named Overback, Cornelius and Weigh from the Munich school. Their creative natures had been able to communicate with the mystical by using the pagan and the natural but not by being used by them. He vastly approved of such paintings as Overbeck's 'Sponsalizio', Cornelius's 'Last Judgment' and others of the same genre. Such works of art alone had been able to catch the spirit that was so essential.

In other words, it was the German school of artists who understood that good art required the proper philosophical base. To Wiseman, art that was merely artistic was, at best, representational. Of course it would be argued that all artists had personal philosophical premises upon which they operated, but if they were based on something that did not come from the Christian tradition and philosophy, they were deluding themselves into believing they were truly creative. Artists had too long begged the essential question, allowing the geometrical and the harmonious to dominate, in the belief that these were satisfactory substitutes. Alternatively, if they had not allowed the geometrical and the harmonious to prevail they had failed to search for internal inspiration. For too long they had been involved with a love of beauty and had not properly been concerned with a perception of natural beauty. Certainly, they had reflected nature, they had captured the best elements of the classical tradition — Wiseman does not deny them these virtues — but they had not seen with 'pure eyes'. To use a latter nineteenth-century impressionist artist Cezanne as an example, it can be seen that he gradually escaped from the purely natural to the essentially geometrical, but in specific terms, he fails as an artist because he lacks the essential element of religious faith in the portrayal of his subject. He is permitted by God to have a partial vision, but the final result of his artistic impulse is unsatisfactory because his soul never manages to achieve harmony with the divine.

All of this is a preliminary to what Wiseman would define as proper Christian art. In his *Recollections of the Last Four Popes* he describes what is not Christian art and, therefore, by definition, is bad art. The 'Barocco' in architecture, the 'Berniniesque' in sculpture, and 'Mannerism' in painting, and also 'the cold classical school . . . of which David was the type in France, . . . ; which sought its subjects in an unclean mythology or a pagan heroism . . .'[22] The key phrases here are 'unclean mythology' and 'a pagan heroism' for these obviously do not reflect the natural love rising to the supernatural. Indeed, he really castigates this 'cold classical school' still further by stating that their colours are raw and unmellow, 'overbright and unbending, devoid of delicacy and tenderness. . . .'[23] The essence of Christian love is tenderness; the classical tradition excludes this feeling and also lacks what Wiseman would define as a sense of natural beauty. He believed that the 'cold classical school' at best slavishly copied the ancient tradition but did not really emulate its particular spirit, limited though that spirit was.

Wiseman was sure that although what he called Christian art was to be found in Europe, it was relatively unknown in England. His explanation was based on the fact that the English Roman Catholic community, in its isolated state from continental traditions, had itself not experienced artistic elements which come with the religious ceremonial. Moreover, in England and to a degree elsewhere, real knowledge of any true form of Christian art had not been readily available. The cheap prints of a popular nature which were easily obtainable and which passed for Christian art were without a sense of religious purpose and essential creative spirit. With the appearance of good copies of Christian art, the result would be that people would discover for themselves how long they had been deluded in accpeting poor imitations.

In an attempt to put the matter precisely, he asked two questions: 'Where is Christian art?' and 'Does it merely copy earlier masterpieces?' To the latter query the answer was in the negative; to the former, the answer was that it was the new German school — better known as the Nazarenes — which flourished in Munich and Düsseldorf. This art was 'not only blooming with sweet grace, but is gradually shedding its seed on fertile ground around it, repaying in Christian beauty, the classical accuracy which fed its own roots.'[24] It should be noted that Wiseman allowed classical origins provided they were based on true nature and not on slavish reproduction of the antique.

Therefore it was not mere accuracy that was significant, but there had to be an 'accordance between the expression and ideas and sentiments which his [the observer's] heart tells him are good and holy.'[25] Christian art, the only real art, ensures that there is no doubt as to subject matter. The true spirituality of the holy figure is expressed in 'dignity of attitude, nobleness of features, holiness of expression, majesty of action.'[26] The function of art is to emphasize natural arrangement and an uncomplicated *mise en scene*. Beauty is thereby meaningful and apprehended by the observer. The resulting picture almost exhudes 'holy calm, and quiet beauty' [27] with a sense of seeing and apprehending exactly and, in a literal sense, what each person portrayed is saying and thinking.

But he was willing to recognize that all creative art is not identical. He recognized that painting differed from architecture; to him the latter was less imaginative or original. Indeed, he believed that architecture tended to revert to older models because the public was less willing to experiment in this genre. They could see a building, utilize its functions and be directly involved, whereas with a picture they would be involved but in a different sense. Christian pictorial art must promote a greater sense of spiritual love which an architectural creation is not necessarily designed to do, although it may, as evinced in the great mediaeval cathedrals.

Proper Christian art should 'not look at time, but at nature, which changes not. . . .' [28] However, one should not assume that the middle ages necessarily saw the highest form of art. Artistic incompetence has been often canonized for itself alone, with distortion, the grotesque and unnatural forms being retained because they were deemed to be mystical or symbolic. As Wiseman wryly noted: 'We have seen representations of saints such as we honestly declare we should be sorry to meet in flesh and blood, with the reality of their emblematic sword or club about them, on the highway at evening', [29] such art says little that is really meaningful to the eye or the feelings. Emotionally it is empty. 'It is to be desired and aimed at, that the beholder, antiquarian or simple, scholar or peasant, should at once feel himself penetrated with a sense of the beautifully holy, be enamoured of the virtues which beam from the face, and seem to clothe the form of the figure before him; that from earthly comeliness his thoughts should rise to the contemplation of heavenly charms; that he should weep or exult, be humbled or gain confidence, as he gazes — not to study or criticize, but to feel.' [30] Many a modern art critic, both amateur and professional would agree with such sentiments, that is, with regard to 'feeling' rather than 'reason'.

According to Wiseman, the artist had to provide the 'truth' which, in the portrayal of the human form, meant that there had to be the essential muscles and bones. Despite a penchant for the traditional in theology, he did not like the mediaeval approach or pseudo-mediaeval approach of delineating 'a body haggard, if not ill-favoured countenance; . . .' [31] Of course, devotees of this tradition would reply to Wiseman that this somehow emphasized the mystical; but he would refuse to accept this argument. The Byzantine school, which he had totally rejected as being hard and over-formalized, had just such characteristics.

How could Christian art be realized? Wiseman suggested that far from being antiquarian, 'it must start on the principle that it is essentially a creative art, that it must invent; it must not servilely copy; . . . it may imitate but not transcribe. . . .'[32] In the recent past, Christian art often just copied: now it must begin anew. He insisted that an artist must be able to draw from nature, but at the same time gradually assume the sentiments 'which belong to religion as distinct from nature, and to the inward, rather than to the outward life.'[33] Here may be the key: he had required that the artist do more than merely reflect; he must also enter the soul.

With that special confidence that imbued the nineteenth century and in spite of not being an artist himself, next he proposed how this Christian art was to be brought into reality. Firstly, the artist must study what Wiseman would call Roman Catholic art; secondly, he must use as a model that individual or item which somehow managed to reflect in itself the image to be portrayed; and lastly, the artist himself must be imbued with what he designated the spirit. However, this did not mean a simple appreciation of natural beauty, for naturalism alone is cold. He demanded more than a natural delineation, a sanctity of delineation. The artist must be a religious man; a man who would 'work with faith and for love, whose outward performances will be only counterparts of an inward devotion', and the subjects realized 'shall be the visions of their own pious meditations, and the fruit of their constant conversation with things spiritual and holy.'[34]

The age-old problem of ascertaining why an artist creates, Wiseman faced boldly. He rejected the idea that the artist worked for his own satisfaction alone, although he allowed that the artist's personal desires and wishes to express himself were important. The true artist should paint for the people. Wiseman demanded that public taste be recognized; and if a picture were unsatisfactory to the public at large, he judged it a failure. It might be argued that this view is just pandering to a passing sense of taste and represents judgement at the lowest possible artistic level, but then he was sure that 'the people' had an innate sense of what is right. In his view, the artist must be able to utilize in his art things which say to the beholder what is truly significant, but at the same time he must not make his art too difficult to comprehend. In the highest artistic creation, there are no doubts as to meaning. To project, the composition need not be complicated; to illustrate his point he referred to a painting by Herbert exhibited in the Royal Academy in 1847, which showed Christ in the workshop of Joseph with His family. Wiseman declared that this picture was original

82

yet at the same time able to express the universal, and he noted that each 'figure is apart, detached, so as to claim, and actually receive separate and successive attention.' [35] The painting is accurate, the background is satisfactory but not demanding particular attention. The picture expresses total religious sentiment and the observer is fully involved with all the persons portrayed. As his highest form of praise Wiseman says: 'It required no book-learning to understand, to comprehend, and to feel it; it cannot make any but one impression, a tender and a devout one; . . .' [36] He also took this occasion to make a comment on Turner: the latter's work was described as having a 'ghastly brilliance' and being 'incomprehensible'. Etty, on the other hand, receives some praise, but considerably less than is given to Herbert. To Wiseman, Herbert particularly conveyed deepest religious sentiment and did so by using the highest creative powers. Religious art was a 'creative power', 'not . . . a servile imitator' of past forms, traditional or otherwise. Even in what he often called 'this degenerate age' Herbert was able to find 'subjects not treated before, and [made] them fit vehicles for the conveying to the mind of believers most religious impressions.'

Although the artist is a creative individual and must not be bound to the past, Wiseman believed that there were certain artistic conventions or canons which must be obeyed. For example, religious figures often carry traditional symbols which help to make the pictures more intelligible, enabling the observer to absorb the feelings engendered by the work of art. Moreover, the artist should not capriciously deck out his subjects just for 'high art'. There are traditional garbs which have the same effect as the symbols, for it is incongruous to imagine certain subjects totally out of their proper ambience. Ironically enough, however, many Renaissance artists, many of whose works Wiseman approved, did not hesitate to show religious scenes in local rather than middle eastern situations. Yet his general comments can be shown to apply in two instances as examples; the first in the large nude statue of Napoleon and the second in the statute of Washington in a toga. The mind boggles at the incongruity of having such subjects so portrayed. Indeed, the classical tradition of David is also illustrative of the same line of argument. Nudity is pagan, classical and, hence, sinful; moreover, it is not an essential feature of great art. Drapery added a sense of form, a sense of completeness and allowed for the greater use of line. Wiseman felt that good art was often rich in colour, partly because there were traditional colours associated with religious figures, and because he was frequently unappreciative of subtle and delicate shadings.

It should perhaps be pointed out anew that Wiseman did not like Byzantine art. To him this school of art was just too rigid, too conventional and, too imitative. He really thought the Byzantine school was the exemplification of the dangers which would come if nineteenth-century artists did not become creative as he defined the process. Religious artists all too frequently repeated old themes in an unimaginative fashion and this, carried out to the extreme, created the unfulfilling Byzantine style.

What was the reaction of the public to good religious art? Wiseman said that, given proper examples, people would respond favourably. He felt that this had already happened to a limited degree. 'What is called the Pre-Raphaelite school has arisen, and made a progress, which may one day, under the religious influences, which it clearly wants, become the germ of a truly Christian school of art. At present, with some exceptions, it stands to real Christian art as the works of Niccolo di Fuligno do to those of Beato Angelico.' Since the majority of his own British contemporaries had never been abroad, Wiseman was convinced that they had never seen real religious art, or any good art at all for that matter.

To rectify this situation he suggested that the English ought to acquire works of art from the continent and in particular from Germany. He admired Overbeck especially and he proposed that contemporary British artists would do well to emulate his work. However, whatever was done must not be small and inadequate: 'We must begin with something great and noble at once,' he noted. Christian art must not come out before the public, for the first time, mean and imperfect.' Early efforts must remain essentially private and it is only after much experimentation and great care that the results should be exhibited, for nothing is less satisfactory than noble experimentation and effort which fails. Moreover, since the public were already so jaundiced and depraved in their tastes, a situation which was not entirely their own fault, to show them imperfect Christian art, that is to say good art improperly conceived, would be disastrous.

His own view of art was dominated not only by the fact that he was a professed Christian, but also by virtue of his being a member of the Roman Catholic Church. He was sincerely convinced that no Protestant could produce real Christian art and that the Protestant tradition *per se* was against art. He observed that 'Protestantism, as regards art, is essentially unholy. . . .' [37] If, as in protestant art, you 'disconnect' holiness from pictorial art, you end up with 'masses of gross flesh and most unsaintly countenance' [38] as in the co-called religious art of Rubens. Moreover, by denying the 'mythos' of the mediaeval world, the protestant tradition had

84

destroyed it as an artistic conception. He also implied that the Anglican artist, for example, instead of vesting St. Cuthbert or St. Thomas in cope and mitre, would dress 'the Anglo-Saxon bishop in lawn sleeves and wig'; he would garb attendant angels 'in a chorister's surplice' and adoring clergy 'in the cap and gown of a university proctor. . . .'[39] This is very harsh and in a way denies what Wiseman had said earlier about perception.

He was convinced that good are would arise like the phoenix, given the right ambience and *weltanschauung*. He believed that there were many talented young artists able to create the long desired good art, but that they required the proper inspiration; the Roman Catholic artist alone had this inspiration because from his church alone came the spiritual guidance essential for good art. Art was not necessarily entirely religious; secular art was acceptable, but both sacred and profane art had to be the object of divine inspiration and be created by the proper perception of 'natural beauty'.

Wiseman was much addicted to the work of the German school; but Spain also produced art to his satisfaction, for the obvious reasons. With 'the exception of the royal painters, whose works were not exposed to commercial risks, the Spanish artists devoted themselves almost entirely to the service of the Church.'[40] It was not painters alone who were so limited in their activity, for the architect also tended to put his talents chiefly to the building of various religious edifices; 'the sculptor . . . [did not desecrate] his chisel by producing lascivious, or even profane forms but laboured his life long on sacred images. . . .'[41] Spanish art was not a commercial activity but a religious one designed for a particular purpose and it was only after the French invasion that Spanish works of art were seen outside their traditional settings. Wiseman disapproved of what had occurred later; he felt mystic art was not suited to galleries and he thought Spanish art in particular looked dull and uninspired in most museums.

In Wiseman's view, Spanish art never became truly secular in the Italian sense (parenthetically it should be noted that he nowhere mentions Goya) and much to his satisfaction Spain never had 'a profane or to speak more tenderly, a *classical* school of art; a school of nudities, that is, of mythologies, of heathenism, and of the vices.'[42] He was aware, however, that even in Spain there was some non-religious art and he believed that it came out of the romantic tradition; he was convinced, though, that in Spain it was not overly significant. It was evident that 'painting has remained, in Spain, true to her maiden love of the celestial alone; . . . she has disdained aught less elevated than the glory of God and His

85

Saints.' [43] The national art of Spain had these well ordered and comprehended bases; the direction of thought had been conjoined with religion as the unifying force. [44]

On the other hand, Wiseman was certain that in the England of his day there was no school of painting. He did not deny that there were competent and even brilliant artists such as Landseer and Stanfield, but they were unique. In general, Wiseman denigrated the British portrait tradition, saying of it: 'Our portrait painters make likenesses but not pictures.' [45] This last statement is somewhat contradictory for in his *Recollections of the Last Four Popes*, he is filled with praise for Lawrence's portrait of Pius VII. Of course, it may well be that the subject rather than the artist himself in this instance was the cause of the success of this work. Even the historical pictures he felt were inadequate because the spirit which inspired them was purely secular. But there were signs of change which he welcomed. With the erection of the parliament buildings at Westminster, the government was becoming a new patron and, to Wiseman, this was the initial attempt to establish a national school; but, of course, he thought its future was bleak unless it was divinely inspired. [46] He doubted whether it was possible for an artist to 'reach grandeur in depicting the real' without fully involving himself 'with enthusiasm from the ideal.' [47] It is clear from earlier remarks what his 'ideal' was; to summarize 'the union of beauty with purity; and the union of sorrow with divinity.' [48] He feared that if the contemporary British were to attempt a school of art without such a basis there could never be the 'graceful and sublime abstraction of beauty.' [49] It should not be thought, however, that mere sorrow and mere pain can achieve the essence of perception, for alone they 'are opposed to the natural estimate of the sublime.' [50] The classical artist might portray these emotions, that is, 'mere sorrow and mere pain,' but he could not ennoble them because these artists lacked 'the conception of the truth . . . the extreme of griefs borne as none but God could bear them.' [51] Consequently, because the British could only observe the mystical art, know about it intellectually and have a 'mere artistic or romantic enthusiasm' for it, they could not produce true art. Wiseman felt that, consequently, the proposed British national historical school of painting would not succeed because both the artists and the society lacked the fundamental religious experience. Because the subject matter of so much that is good in art is historical in nature, and because religion and history are interwoven, there can be no real art that neglects true religion. It was precisely here, Wiseman felt, that art in Britain failed, for religion and history were not truly enmeshed. Traditions, which to Wiseman were

86

sacred, had been discarded by the reformation with the result that much art which pretended to be religious in inspiration and even in subject matter was neither. The true mystical spirit was lacking because the artist neither knew nor felt anything of it, and the subject lacked it because it was simply factually wrong and spiritually empty. The intellectual inspiration failed, also, because too few artists had ever had the chance to observe the truth. Wiseman would approve of an artist going to the desert to paint something like 'The Scapegoat', for example, for the basic landscape would be factually correct and would reflect the sense of the subject if not its true religious essence which was outside the artist's experience unless he were a Roman Catholic. Such a position underscored another of his convictions, namely, that until 'the Church Universal' was restored, mankind was living only a partial existence.

Moreover, he also questioned whether pictures which were inspired by the head rather than the heart could 'recollect' the true essentials. The first essential was that true artists painted for the people and that art on a large scale had to be 'simple and intelligible'.[52] The second essential assumed the Aristotelian concept that art could never glorify a bad cause, regardless of the individual virtue in that cause. 'Men should be taught that no amount of heroism, or of individual excellence can sanction a cause which is wrong in principle, and so citiated in its very root.'[53] One must constantly remember 'that painting teaches the same precepts or moral conduct as philosophy.'[54] Art retains its vitality as long as it is promoting moral progress, and it cannot do this without true inspiration, which comes only from the mystical and not from the classical alone. Wiseman doubted that the English could ever have true art because, in their present state of mind, they were not in harmony with the perceptions of spirit which creates it. Having limited great painting to religious painting, with the latter only possible if inspired by the true Christian tradition, he was also convinced that the English, being outside this tradition, would have to settle for lesser art. Their Protestantism doomed them to barren art because they lacked the inherent qualities which come from the Roman Catholic spirit.

Much of the general commentary on painting applied to sculpture as well. The classical tradition was limited to 'the beauty and power of the human form', with the best classical sculpture 'being a dignified repose and the total absence of all muscular effort.'[55] The Christian artists, knowing that nakedness was associated with sin, clothed their figures, and their draperies — as Wiseman calls them — served as 'a mystical veil, translucent, yet impenetrable, revealing

all [the body's] motions, but hiding its form . . . as the sign is sur-
passed by the thing signified. . . .' [56] He aptly summed up Christian
sculpture as 'the ideal circle, circumscribed by a line without
breadth or thickness, [which] surpasses in perfection the rude
diagram by which it is figured forth.' [57] Alas, sculpture was cor-
rupted in the high renaissance because it became too secular and
the pagan traditions reasserted themselves over the mystical. In due
course, sculpture became more and more decadent as it evolved
into the baroque and the roccoco, from which it was only rescued
by Canova and by Thorwaldson. The letter, according to Wiseman,
was a real genius and although he was not a Roman Catholic, he
was somehow inspired by that spirit that Wiseman ordinarily
associated only with Roman Catholics.

How does he feel about architecture? He is one with Pugin,
generally, in feeling that British architecture had declined since
the Reformation. He often thought that the construction of public
buildings in his own time was done at price per yard or so much
per unit and not by any inspired artistic form of entity; utility
rather than sentiment was in command. Wiseman approved,
though, of what was denominated as 'pointed architecture' and he
recommended that any new Roman Catholic churches erected
should use this style since it was based on the right precepts.[58] In
other words, Wiseman supported the neo-mediaevalism. With
proper buildings inevitably would come proper accoutrements,
although Wiseman would hardly have much liked Pugin's remark
to a cleric 'whose sacerdotal dress did not come up to his mediaeval
ideal: "What is the use, my dear sir, in praying for the conversion
of England in a cope like that?" ' [59] Wiseman was somewhat less
rigid and his soul was not, as was Pugin's, fixed in the middle ages.
He had himself lived in Rome, and while he had great admiration
for the basilica as a style, he believed that in his own day the so-
called 'pointed-style' was probably more appropriate. Indeed, one
of Pugin's greatest successes was St. George's, Southwark, which
Wiseman had opened on 4 July 1848; here was a neo-Gothic
church much esteemed not only by Roman Catholics but by perceptive persons of taste throughout the country. The new parliament buildings at Westminster were also in harmony with his basic
precepts on architecture. He always insisted that since his fellow
countrymen were erecting 'the most sumptuous building in Europe
. . . [they should] ensure perfection to the work, . . . [by borrowing]
every detail, as well as every feature and proportion, from those
columniated [mediaeval] ages; so . . . no spire, or tracery, or buttress, or niche, or canopy, or crochet or jamb, or panel, or boss, or
bit of metal-work has been admitted, which could not be justified

by monastic, or ecclesiastical models of Catholic times.'[60] This is Puginism and the Gothic revival with a vengeance.

It is clear that what was truly desired in painting, sculpture and architecture was a form that was inspired by 'the ideal' which in its own turn originated with God. 'Nature is the true foundation of art, and art only its representation.' Wiseman hoped that in his own day there would be a revival of Christian art. It should be said that he did not think that all mystic art had a biblical or religious ethos but he did believe that it should not be antithetical to the Christian spirit. Art should not express purely pagan or naturalistic traditions as it was so prone to do where the protestant reformation had cut off the real source of Christian spirit, that is, the mediaeval Roman Catholic tradition. Of course, hoping as he always did for a national conversion of the English to Roman Catholicism, Wiseman felt that art would then be imbued with the historical tradition and that there would be a renewed connection with the mystical spirit. On a more mundane level, he did believe that art would improve, at least if his fellow countrymen would emulate the Nazarene school. In a sense this occurred in a limited fashion with the Pre-Raphaelites who did follow some of the precepts of the Nazarenes. Nevertheless, Wiseman was not uncritical of the works produced by some of the Pre-Raphaelites because he felt that they failed to apply their own precepts adequately.

Wiseman was a man of his own time but he was not a slave to popular tastes. He liked the mediaeval and early renaissance works of art, and he expressed sentiments that reflected some of the ideas on art held by the Prince Consort. The latter collected pictures which many of his contemporaries found bizarre. Many of their contemporaries failed to understand the mystical spirit that both found appealing; the Victorian's enthusiasm for anecdotal painting made it impossible for him to appreciate the significance of these earlier works.

Taste is a highly personalized entity and thus he felt quite free in making his own judgments even if they were not always in harmony with the views held by his contemporaries. He felt that his experience and his education gave him a special right to help improve — as he saw it at least — the level of are in his own day. He used his position to promote his ideas in a didactic fashion for he saw art teaching moral lessons. He felt that if he educated his audience they would appreciate good art and comprehend its particular moral values.

Perhaps his aims could be summed up as what he hoped for from art. It 'is clear that every advance in correctness of design, beauty, and harmony of colour, and above all in perfection of expression, would please, naturally, even those who could not discover the cause of their emotions, or would only increase and deepen those feelings which the same subject inferiorly treated had before produced.' [61] We 'now desire . . . to see . . . simplicity of action, naturalness of arrangements, and power of expression, which enable the eye to read them, and the feelings to apprehend them — the truest test of real religious art.' [62]

4

Fabiola — The Ideal Sunday Book

Clerical authors in the nineteenth century are ubiquitous, and no form of literary creation in either prose or verse escapes them. Thus, to say that the novel *Fabiola* was written by a person in holy orders is to observe nothing in particular, but *Fabiola* is unique in that its author was not merely an ecclesiastic but an archbishop and a cardinal as well. It is true that Newman wrote novels but these were literary creations of youth and early middle age and written long before he became a cardinal himself.

It is always interesting to speculate why a novel is written. To be sure, there is the old cliché that everyone has a novel in him but few bother to write it, but this is hardly a very satisfactory answer to the query. Today it may seem somewhat eccentric for a man who was a Prince of the Church to have bothered to write a novel. Cardinals seem to be concerned with higher things and one imagines them thinking only of highly theological questions or of church policy. They should not appear to pander to lower tastes; but it must be recollected that the Victorian novel did serve other functions than that of mere entertainment. By the middle of the nineteenth century the novel was a major form, not only artistically, but as a vehicle to convey particular ideas; it had replaced the long narrative poem such as was popular earlier, as well as serious writing for the theatre which had fallen out of fashion. The creative literary artist with something significant to say used the novel, knowing that in this way the largest audience would be reached.

Not all who became novelists were particularly skilful, and many could hardly be considered to be artistically creative individuals. Numerous writers were obsessed with a cause from which originated the essential message. If the cause were insignificant or the writing uninspired, as it so often was, the result was lamentable. Rows and rows of nineteenth-century 'problem' novels now repose in libraries, totally unread; they are the memorials to industry and to an enthusiasm. Domestic censorship often determined whether a book was acceptable, and, of course, there were categories of books which were permitted in some households and not in others. For example, in certain evangelical families a liking for any novel was thought to indicate low morals, and readings them was a vice.

In other households, there were 'Sunday books' which pious parents allowed their offspring to read on the sabbath, while other forms of fiction were taboo. Clerical authors were very much in demand for the 'Sunday books' for it was felt that their writings would ensure the tone on the Lord's day. There was a class and sex bias as well; there were love stories designed for servant girls, and *risqué* 'French' tales for the aristocratic smoking room. Many a middle-class family could approve of a Dickens but not of a Bulwer. All novelists were undoubtedly bound by certain conventions because Podsnapery was very much in evidence; relations between the sexes were handled with the utmost discretion, and the dictum about including nothing that would bring a blush to a maiden's cheek was almost a shibboleth for publishers. The good were to be rewarded, the bad punished, and forgiveness was only possible if sins were confessed and repentance was sincere. An edifying deathbed scene was highly desirable, and the fatherless or motherless child accepting the dictum of Divine providence in a good Christian fashion found almost universal approbation. It was an essential requirement that novels be pure, for British mothers and daughters had to be protected. A knowledge of evil could and did probably come after marriage, but until that time purity was the watchword and, while popular authors might tackle questionable subjects, they did so in such a fashion that Mrs. Grundy would have no cause to complain. Although religious themes were popular, excessive sectarianism was much less so; all that was deemed necessary was an essential Christian spirit. Heterodoxy and Jacobinical philosophy were both rejected. One should hasten to say that all literary works were not escapist or moral tracts. Many novels had as their venue the more sordid aspects of society; Dickens did not hesitate to set his novels far from the salubrious suburbs, nor did Elizabeth Gaskell. The realistic author was merely retelling what was published in the newspapers almost every day and even the most protected could not fail to be aware of conditions among the poor. The grim statements in the numerous governmental reports on working conditions in factories and mines, the horrors of child labour, the tragedies of the chimney sweep and the like, were known to the public. Moreover, and this is part of the Victorian paradox, journals did not hesitate to accept articles on slums, disease, crime or prostitution, but many novelists often pretended that a contrary situation existed, or at least peopled their fictional world in an unreal way, with the result that their characters were only one-dimensional. The reader knew reality in the largest sense but frequently rejected it if described in fictional form. For example, it was evident that all women were not pure and virtuous,

92

but the satisfactory heroine was almost universally so described, with the result that to a modern reader these characters are saccharine and excessively sentimental. Heroes are always manly, honest and upright although society knew that men often acted in a different fashion in every-day life. Secondary characters were often more real; even villains were more human than heroes. Although their evil nature had to be exaggerated, at least they were more than pasteboard.

The novelist who set his story outside the contemporary scene was less shackled by convention. What might be deemed to be improper in Victorian England could be rationalized as an indication of an earlier age's lack of morality, and if a novel were set in the remote past — say classical antiquity — even more license was allowed, since very few had any real idea how such a society actually lived. In addition, to many the antique world was by nature evil — evil in the sense that it was non-Christian — and characters of that time simply could not be expected to act as Christian men and women did in the nineteenth century. Good and evil could also be delineated more easily and more realistically, with the hero and the villain recognizable as individuals and not merely as symbols of virtue or vice. In addition, in the historical novel unpleasant events or situations could be described more graphically since they had no immediate connection with the present.

An author who wrote historical novels had to be careful however. While readers would permit some anachronisms which might be necessary for the plot, they were not uncritical, and a wise author often consulted proper historical sources to ensure accuracy, with the result, as Pooh Bah observed, that writers were able 'to provide artistic verisimilitude to an otherwise bald and unconvincing narrative.'

One great asset of the historical novel was that it was not necessarily subject to present mores and conventions. Aspects of the novel which the critic might find unacceptable if set in the contemporary scene were excused by the venue of time and place. With the past highly romanticized or, alternatively, presented as grim and sordid, the present was either the highest form of progress or in the final stages of decay. In any case, the historical novelist always possesses the best of all possible worlds, providing escapist literature or the morality tale; the writer is less committed than other novelists, for he is not living in the age about which he writes, and he can get outside his subject and regard it critically or with nostalgia, giving the reader the same choice. The novel about the contemporary scene requires a large sense of involvement since

93

it is the here and now which is inescapable.

The successful historical novelist has a kind of transcendent clairvoyance with which he integrates his story successfully in the past. At the same time, by recreating the past one can express sentiments which would not be permissable or seem sensible if one were dealing literally with the present. The past can also be disguised in such a way that, in fact, it is the present; the problems of the contemporary world can be viewed and considered indirectly and in a fashion that would be unacceptable to the conventions of the present day.

As the nineteenth century progressed, the novel with a thesis, a message or a cause became more and more common. While competent authors could combine artistry and message, lesser ones failed miserably; the former used the novel to pose significant questions and to propound some possible solutions. The incompetent authors lacked the perception and sensitivity to deal with the essential features of a good novel. The thesis is not enough; a good novel must have a quality beyond mere sermonizing and preaching. Only very few managed to attain the ideal consistently.

The eighteenth-century novel, while concerned with morality in many cases, could not be called essentially religious. After 1830 or so, the increased concern for religion in general ensured that there was no shortage of audience for the contemporary thesis novel, and authors were able to concern themselves with underlying questions relating to the Christian faith as well as to more immediate problems. Thus, the author of a religious novel set in an historical framework had certain advantages: he could pose questions and require the characters to resolve problems which were similar to those faced by the contemporary world but which would have been considered too contentious if seen only through contemporary eyes. In addition, certain philosophical discussions could be introduced, for example, in a dialogue between pagan and Christian, which could highlight current moral problems but not necessarily label them with party or denomination. Fnally, the religious novel, unless it was excessively sectarian, was safe reading for all the family of any denomination. However, its success depended on its being more than a mere tract which might bore, rather than edify its readers. Some *élan* was required, and religion spiced with action from the past by characters whom one might or might not know socially provided the perfect solution.

One further thought on the religious novel set in an historical context: it allowed the author to preach not only his own theology but to teach as well. Many of his descriptions of individuals, events and places could be presented as if by the historian, who dealt with facts. Such a novel was, therefore, acceptable on more than one level; it educated, it entertained and it taught a moral. If well done it could be both convincing and satisfying.

Wiseman's *Fabiola* is not a distinguished novel *per se*, but it was, however, widely read. Its importance is not only as a museum piece of Victoriana but as an indication of certain aspects of Wiseman's thinking, and as an expression of his views on the uses of literature. It has roots in his personal belief that the public was interested in questions of faith and that religion was a compelling part of everyday life.

In a long article which appeared in the *Dublin Review* entitled 'Controversial novels—Geraldine', the reviewer—who incidentally was Wiseman's friend Bagshawe — severely castigated his contemporaries, who according to him were novelists using poor material and, worse still, presenting it badly. He did not say that authors were necessarily incompetent, but rather that their subjects were unworthy. The obvious solution was for the novelist to utilize his talents by selecting better material. He says further: 'We have abundance of materials for them [novels] in the lives of saints, authentic miracles of a later date, in many beautiful legends preserved by the pious, . . . [There] are many subjects which would require little extraneous embellishment, and through which might be infused, into the minds of our children, the full spirit and beauty of Catholicity. Fiction is too strong a weapon to be left to our opponents, we must enlist it on our side; and if we use it with judgment and uprightness, we shall find it of incalculable advantage in attracting the minds and hearts of the young to our holy religion.' Here may well be the origins of *Fabiola*. Bagshawe wanted novels to serve a specific purpose and he was actively promoting the idea that the writer should use religious topics but not necessarily, one should note, matters of doctrine. Literature was like history which was a form of philosophy, teaching by example. While more novels appeared orientated in the direction advocated by Bagshawe, it was not until almost twenty years later that a volume appeared which could be said to fulfil his requirements completely. This was Wiseman's own novel *Fabiola*.

In the last century it was very much *à la mode* for publishers to establish a series of books under one common title; for example, there was Bohn's Classical Library, Routledge's Railway Library and the like. In order to attract the Roman Catholic reader, a series known as the Popular Catholic Library was proposed. As the senior Roman Catholic ecclesiastic, Wiseman was consulted on the plan, gave it his approval and even suggested themes for such a series, namely a collection 'of tales illustrative of the condition of the

95

Church in different periods of her past existence. One, for instance, might be called "The Church of the Catacombs"; a second, "The Church of the Basilicas" — each comprising three hundred years; a third would be on "The Church of the Cloister"; and then, perhaps, a fourth might be added, called "The Church of the Schools." '

In spite of the heavy demands on his time, Wiseman was so enthusiastic about the project that he even volunteered to write one of the first novels of the series. His offer was accepted, but after some thought he asked not to be committed to a date for its completion. From various remarks made by its author, it would appear that the book was begun in the spring of 1854; but progress was far from speedy. The major obstacle was his own incapacity to keep to business at hand — and he never had enough secretarial help — so that the writing of *Fabiola* did not have more than a small portion of his attention or his time.

When the book was finally completed and published, Wiseman himself explained his method of composition; there had been no real overall plan and it had been a slow process. He had worked on it when he was travelling or freed from the pressure of other duties. He believed that it was necessary for the reader to know how the book had been written because otherwise its unevenness might be surprizing. He was well aware that the various parts did not always seem well connected and, although he recognized these failings, he did not explain why he did not revise the text to improve it. He stated that he had enjoyed writing *Fabiola* because it had provided him with an agreeable occupation when his regular work was done and because it was an escape.

In his review some years previously, Bagshawe had indicated that the lives of the saints and beautiful pious legends were the stuff of Roman Catholic literature. Wiseman, taking these suggestions as a directive, wrote accordingly. He provided the 'extraneous embellishment . . . [to] infuse the beauty of Catholicity.' He firmly avowed that what he had not done was to write a learned tome. 'His desire,' he said, 'was rather to make his reader familiar with the usages, habits, conditions, ideas, feeling, and spirit of the early ages of Christianity.' While not necessarily an expert on the period, he had a general familiarity with his material; he was knowledge-able about the martyrs and saints, and he used them as part of the story. He based his plot on the traditional hagiographical accounts and wove them into his narrative. Moreover, being very familiar with the city of Rome, he could describe the place in such a fashion as was realistic enough for his purpose. Because he was writing fiction, he could also take his hagiography literally; there was no necessity to question, even if he had been so inclined. By taking this course he need not apply any of the critical apparatus which was an important part of the historical discipline because such was not an essential element in fiction.

In order to disarm any potential criticism on this score he was careful to emphasize that he had not written a history. He made it abundantly clear that by using the non-academic approach he was able to take liberties with chronology. Indeed, he said that he had done so; however, he also indicated that he had tried to be generally accurate. To give his novel some verisimilitude he had to describe the pagan world in careful and precise language, but he had not felt obliged to relate in detail facts which might not be suitable to his audience. He was aware of the 'pure maiden' and in discussing pagan society he emphasized that its 'worst aspect has been carefully suppressed, as nothing could be admitted here which the most sensitive Catholic eye would shrink from contemplating.' Throughout the novel he was determined to maintain a 'high moral tendency' and thereby counter Bagshawe's strictures on novelists in general. Leslie Stephen would have applauded: 'Remember the country parson's daughters; I have always to remember them.' As a basic subject, Wiseman chose 'the Church of the Catacombs'; 'some admiration and love may be inspired by it of these primitive times, which an over-excited interest in later and more brilliant epochs of the Church is too adpt to diminish or obscure.' By deliberately eschewing his own day he could not be taxed with being partisan; by declining to set his novel in the post-reformation he could escape from undue controversy, and by taking the antique he could express almost any viewpoint he chose. He could not be charged, moreover, with attempting to convert his reader to a particular point of view in the contemporary world. Above all, by choosing 'the Church of the Catacombs' he was being truly 'Catholic' — not merely Roman Catholic — and his story would appeal to all Christians regardless of denomination. While the novel which ensued was not of great literary merit, it achieved its aims and, indeed, might be termed a *succés fou*.

As with so many novels in the nineteenth century, the plot is somewhat complicated and cumbersome as there are several interwoven themes. However, the dominant one is concerned with Fabiola; the sub-plots are reasonably neatly dovetailed into the principal theme and in all, Fabiola plays a significant rôle. Nevertheless, these sub-plots are not essential to the narrative, and if any or all were omitted, the essential story would still be intact. The novel could be described as a study in contrast, in which the daemonic ultimately triumphs over the demonic. Indeed, it is almost classically romantic in the use of imagery to indicate the various forces involved, with the whole concept of the light and the dark, good and evil, being ever-present and consciously so.

Fabiola is the daughter and sole heiress of a rich and indolent widower. Interestingly enough, Wiseman does not describe her looks and appearance directly. This was apparently deliberate, for other characters are described more carefully; their features are reckoned to give a clue to their inner characters. By inference and allusion one gradually receives the impression that Fabiola is very beautiful. She is also clever and well read, but her learning has not made her humble for she is proud and haughty, the *summum bonum* of the Roman patricians. Wiseman particularly emphasized her chastity which plays an ever greater rôle in her life when she finally abandons paganism, for it is this virtuousness which ennobles her as a person and which is the mark of the true Christian.

On the other hand, Agnes, who is Fabiola's cousin, is described specifically as the pure child, but at the same time with a sense of maturity. Certain physical features were emphasized, for example, her eyes are described as being 'dove-like', with an intensity that indicated something beyond this earthly sphere. She had a forehead which was 'the very seat of candour, open and bright with undisguised truthfulness, . . .' and there was an innocence and freshness about her that was very appealing. In sum, she was the very essence of maidenhood, far from having the worldly character of her cousin. It is made clear from the beginning that Agnes is already a secret Christian and it is her marytrdom that is to be one of the means whereby Fabiola becomes converted. Agnes is also wealthy, (in fact she too is an heiress), and is known universally for her kindness and generosity. For her, wealth is a means of doing good, not merely something to be enjoyed. Although there are fundamental differences in character between Agnes and Fabiola, they are extremely intimate, and this is a further demonstration of the former's lovable nature knowing as she does of the hardness of Fabiola's character.

Fabiola has three women slaves, each of whom plays a significant rôle in the story. Afra, whose real name is Jubola, was Numidian or African, her black skin indicating an evil nature. This racist viewpoint was not uncommon in the last century. Moreover, as the descendant of Ham she is inherently of inferior character. At first she is seen only as a flatterer, but later her true nature emerges when she stoops to murder to gain her ends. Graia is a Greek, less evil than Afra — merely dishonest and wily. The third is Syra from Asia; she is modest and unassuming — very like Cordelia in contrast to Goneril and Regan in *King Lear* — and as

98

she is a Christian she does not hesitate to expound her ideas to her mistress.

It is clear from the opening chapters that Syra is to be a very important character. Indeed, she is to be the key figure, not only in the conversion of Fabiola, but also in the complicated plot of identity which seems to be so much a part of Victorian novels. Syra wishes martyrdom too but for one cause, namely, Fabiola's conversion. Among the female characters, only Afra is to play an evil rôle. From the very beginning, much is made of her special arts; not only is she knowledgeable in the making of love potions, but also of poisons. She is a combination of the exotic and the bad; perhaps one is really an attribute of the other. However, none of the female characters actually is as essentially wicked as those of the male sex, for the author reserves pure evil for men; women are inherently more tender.

The male counterpart of Fabiola is Sebastian, a tribune who has a special place within the imperial household. He is about thirty years old, 'handsome in person . . . a perfect specimen of a noble-hearted youth, full of honour and generous thoughts; strong and brave without a particle of pride or display in him.' One might almost say that his nobility and upright character could serve as the model for any virtuous Englishman of the Victorian age. He is the protector of the son of a Christian martyr, a boy named Pancratius, manly, brave and athletic, who idolizes Sebastian. The former is the masculine equivalent of Agnes. Sebastian sometimes plays an ambivalent rôle. He does not hesitate to use his power as tribune to visit two boys who have been imprisoned for their adherence to Christianity. The youths have doubts about their faith, and their families are asking them to recant to save their lives, but Sebastian takes a hand; 'Can this be true which I have heard, that while angels were putting the last flower to your crowns, you have bid them pause, and even thought of telling them to unweave them and scatter their blossoms to the winds? Can I believe that you who have already your feet on the threshold of paradise, are thinking of drawing them back, to tread once more the valley of exile and tears?' In slightly other circumstances and with differing language but echoing similar sentiments the Captain of the School might exhort a Rugby XV facing a highly superior team. His words find the 'true hearts' of the boys and they do not weaken. What is more miraculous is that everyone present, on hearing Sebastian's statement, decides to become Christian too. It is one of the author's privileges to have Sebastian openly converting people to Christianity with total impunity. Of course, the boys and their families were liable to execution, but death in such circumstances almost guarantees them salvation. This scene foreshadows a somewhat similar one later in the novel involving Pancratius.

Pancratius was arrested after performing an act of charity to his fellow Christians. Sebastian had not allowed him to be arrested earlier for an act of rebellion, the removal of an imperial proclamation against the Christians, because this would have made him a hero in the classical sense, that is in the conflict between tyranny and liberty. Sebastian wanted Pancratius to win the martyr's crown for the right reasons and therefore when he was arrested for what Sebastian deemed to be a proper cause he observed: 'When I heard sentence pronounced on you . . . because you are a Christian, and for nothing else, I felt that my task was ended; I would not have raised a finger to save you.' (The prefect to the junior boy who has upheld the honour of the school could hardly have put it better.) Pancratius realizes why Sebastian has acted in such a fashion and he is grateful to him. The youth comprehends that he is heroic, but for the sake of Christ and not for mere bravery. When Pancratius is on the way into the forum and meets Sebastian, the latter says to him: 'Courage, dearest boy; may God bless you! I shall be close behind the Emperor; give me a last look there, and — your blessing.' Sebastian goes even further, he even brings Pancratius' mother Lucenia to witness her son's execution, and she sees in her son's martyrdom the culmination of her hopes. Thus, the classical Roman idea of motherhood is given an extended importance in light of Christian virtue.

Evil is personified in Corvinus, a contemporary of Pancratius. This boy is a real villain, described as 'sottish, coarse and brutal' with a 'bloated and freckled countenance,' and 'blear eyes, one of which was half closed.' Although still young he was dissolute, dissipated, unrefined and above all, he 'had never experienced in himself a generous feeling, and he had never curbed an evil passion.' Even Maximian, the tyrannical emperor observed to Corvinus' father: 'Why, Prefect, I had no idea you had such an ugly son.' Again, the emphasis is on the physical aspect, to delineate character. Corvinus plots with Afra and indeed, with anyone, to get his revenge on his enemies. He is so over-drawn that he is almost the parody of the nineteenth-century villain. He is so lacking in moral fibre that he even takes revenge on old Cassianus, his Christian teacher, who had failed to reward him in what he considered a fitting manner. For this petty reason, Corvinus and some of his cohorts murder the old man by stabbing him with a stylo. As is to be expected, Corvinus meets his just end; he becomes an alcoholic, and finally is filled with remorse at his persecution of Pancratius who had never acted against him and who had also actually saved his life.

The other malevolent character is Fulvius. He came from Asia Minor and was a protégé of the Emperor Diocletian. From all external appearances he was obviously rich and out to make his way. Fulvius is desirous of marrying Agnes and thereby acquiring her fortune because money and position dominate all of his actions. Nevertheless, although he is a schemer, he is not evil. His projects are thwarted by Fabiola, and in a rage — he actually gnashes his teeth — he says: 'Haughty Roman dame! thou shalt bitterly rue this day and hour. Thou shall know how Asia can revenge.' All his actions are really controlled by Euratos, a manservant who is most mysterious but whom Fulvius obviously fears. Fulvius is also a friend of Torquatus who had been converted to Christianity but later has doubts and who subsequently betrays his friends and suffers accordingly. However, he should not be thought of as inherently evil, only as weak.

The novel has all the adventure, violence and romance that made it appealing to the readers of the day. Sebastian is martyred — he is of course St. Sebastian — with arrows but does not die. Fabiola enlists Afra's help to have him and he recovers. He reappears at court, is re-arrested and finally clubbed to death. Pancratius has earlier died a martyr in the forum. Agnes is also arrested; her youth and innocence make an impression on her judges but even so she is found guilty and beheaded immediately after her trial. Christian suffering and humility are an essential element in all of the martyrdoms.

There is also the nice matter of mixed identity. At an early stage in the novel Fabiola, having struck Syra, covers her wound with a silk scarf which Syra had owned prior to becoming a slave. The scarf is dropped and is picked up by Fulvius who recognizes it. Later Fulvius tries to murder Fabiola in a scene that is very much of the period; 'he thrust her violently down upon the couch, and seized her hair. She made no resistance, she uttered no cry, . . . a noble feeling of self-respect checked any unseemly exhibition of fear before a scornful enemy.' However, Syra intervenes, and it is then discovered that she is Fulvius' sister called Miriam, but during his attack on Fabiola, Fulvius' dagger has struck and mortally wounded his sister.

This noble gesture of Syra is sufficient to cause Fabiola to become a Christian; Syra, or Miriam, is now at peace. On her deathbed she tells Fabiola her story. She came from Antioch and was the daughter of a rich man who lost his fortune. Euratos is her uncle while Fulvius, her brother, is really called Orontius. The two men had plotted to take Miriam's small inheritance which had miraculously not vanished when her father's money disappeared, both Euratos and Fulvius having lost their share in the debacle. They were successful in obtaining Miriam's fortune, and now, penniless, she decided to leave Antioch and go to Jerusalem. But followed by misfortune, she was shipwrecked, sold into slavery and in due course came into Fabiola's household. Despite all Fabiola's efforts to the contrary, Miriam does not long survive and dies a holy death, but is happy that her erstwhile mistress has become a Christian.

There is a nice tidy coda to explain what happens afterwards. The reader is not just left at Miriam's deathbed with Fabiola a Christian, but the story is continued into the reign of Constantine to the year 318. Agnes's tomb had become a shrine as had those of Pancratius and Sebastian. Corvinus, much older and now an alcoholic, accidentally releases a caged tiger, is himself attacked and dies of hydrophobia. Torquatas, repenting his betrayal, now works for Fabiola; even Orontius reappears having expiated his sins. He tells how he and Euratas fled from Rome and how the latter tried to poison him. The poison had been acquired earlier from Afra but, by a fluke, the stronger vial was consumed by Euratas. Afra emerges from the crowd and tells how she gave Euratas the two vials and that the smaller one was really the weaker potion. Euratas had actually intended to murder his nephew as he knew one vial was stronger but made the error as to which it was. Just at this moment Afra or Jubola as she is properly called, is hit with an arrow shot by her husband who is in the guard, but before she experies she too becomes a Christian. Orontius and Fabiola pray at Miriam's tomb; Orontius then departs for a life of an anchorite in Baza and Fabiola continues to do good works and dies at an advanced age as a pious Christian. Miriam, or Syra, has brought Orontius and Fabiola to God; her death was not in vain.

Wiseman manages to complete his moral tale in a neat and thoroughly satisfactory manner. The good are rewarded, either with salvation after martyrdom or following penance and living the new life. All the evil characters are properly punished.

Aside from the highly edifying plot, the novel also includes a series of interpolations of a purely historical nature. In one chapter entitled 'A Talk with the Reader' Wiseman gives a general account of the history of persecutions of the Church and the position of the Christians in the late Roman Empire. It sets the story in context, giving it a verisimilitude which enhances the narrative generally. In other chapters Wiseman describes the catacombs and even includes some examples of inscriptions found there. He explains the use of the term 'catacomb' itself and how it came to be used. He is

102

careful, precise and accurate in these historical interpolations and once more provides elucidation for his readers. He knows they are not scholars, and although this material is not essential to the plot, it does give an authenticity to his story. He wishes to ensure that the reader, while not only appreciating the significance of the moral tale, is also being educated. Elsewhere he carefully describes the city of Rome, the architecture of the basilica, the method of arming the imperial guard, early ordination, communion ceremonies and the like; all these asides are factually correct. Occasionally he even provides footnotes giving as his sources Eusebius or the *Acta Martyri*; he also provides little sketches of such items as the subterranean church in the cemetery of St. Agnes, and gives an explanation of the pronunciation of names. In sum, this is no mere novel but something rather more.

Stylistically, the writing is a curious mixture. Syra, for example, talks like a highly educated cleric while Sebastian's language is a combination of head-boy and the school missioner. All the Christians tend to speak in an unnatural fashion, best described as clerical. In the straight expository sections one almost feels as if one is reading a sermon: 'Earnest was the prayer, earnest the gaze of the eye of heaven, earnest the listening of the ear for the welcoming strain of the heavenly porters. . . .' Other parts read as if they were written by one of the many novelists of the day catering to the lowest possible literary taste. Those sections which can be considered as purely historical, and not essential to the plot, are written in the good solid prose of the nineteenth century, which makes it all the more regrettable that the author failed to use similar language throughout his work. However, these vagaries did not strike his contemporaries as being egregious; he was not alone in using such a mixture of styles.

The difficulty in considering the novel seriously is that it is too much of a tract. At the drop of a hat, everyone is able to discourse on theological subjects either pagan or Christian. The author is not a novelist; he has a few good moments it is true, and the general plot is not bad, but the overall effect is much too moralizing. However, although the novel glorifies the Roman Catholic tradition, it does so within the whole canon of the Christian Church. There is nothing which is essentially sectarian; it is propaganda but not proselytizing.

A not too dissimilar novel, written by John Henry Newman and entitled *Callista*, appeared in the year after *Fabiola* was published. Interestingly enough, Wiseman was perturbed lest the new book affect the sales of his own work, but this did not occur. Indeed, Wiseman's novel did much better than Newman's despite the latter's more competent plotting and better style. *Callista* was less sensational and hence less likely to have a wide interest.

Callista, like *Fabiola*, is set in the third century but somewhat earlier. The action takes place in North Africa. The heroine, Callista, is a Greek whose ultimate conversion and final martyrdom are, naturally enough, the significant elements in the story. Callista is not rich — indeed she paints idols for a living — and is moderately attractive. The secondary plot, however, really dominated the tale. It is the account of Agellius, a rustic youth in his twenties, a Christian of sorts in search of salvation. His religious faith is not too secure, and at times it appears as if he is a Christian merely out of obstinacy, his father having been converted and his family merely followed along. Agellius is protected by his uncle Jucundus who owns the business where Callista is employed. Jucundus is a pagan but a good man and is perhaps the best-drawn character in the novel. Juba, who is the brother of Agellius, is a sort of Toroquatus figure, being ambivalently both for and against the hero and heroine. Juba is the one who really suffers most in the end for he goes mad following an apparent possession by evil spirits. He hardly deserves this fate since he does a number of good things such as saving St. Cyprian who is disguised under the name of Cacillius. The principal villainous character is a witch named Burta, but evil is really personified by the system of society and the world at large, rather than by specific individuals in the book. The Church has grown corrupt and people have sold themselves for the easy life. Surprisingly, perhaps, Newman portrays the pagans as generally decent people. In the novel there is relatively pagans as generally decent people. In the novel there is little bloodshed; a graphic account of the riot in Sicca and the ultimate lynching of a pastry cook is the closest it comes to it. (It is said that Newman drew on his experiences in the 'No Popery' demonstrations for this part of his work.) Callista is tortured, she dies and, following her martyrdom, the novel ends with a Christian burial service conducted by Cyprian in a cave. Indeed, the whole novel is without much action and is very muted in tone, a decided contrast to *Fabiola*.

Although Newman was a better novelist than Wiseman, even his characters periodically talk like theological students involved in a high-level disputation; but this occurs less frequently than in *Fabiola*. Newman, like Wiseman, has the same habit of giving explanations of classical allusions: he translates all the Latin tags in footnotes thus adding a historical note to the work as a whole. By so doing he is also able to emphasize his own scholarship and underline the historical accuracy of his work. The writing is less lush and overdrawn than that of Wiseman, and perhaps this is an indication of the essential difference between the two men.

Newman in his 'Advertisements' emphasizes that he is not writing a history but that his work is purely fictitious. He also points out that, as a book, it has no 'pretensions to an antiquarian character'. He does admit that he has done some research, more 'than may appear at first sight', and in a postscript written in February 1856 indicates how the book came to be written. Chapters I, IV and V plus the story of Juba were written in 1848 — apparently when he was also composing *Loss and Gain* — but after this much was completed, he stopped for lack of inspiration. He revived his interest seven years later and completed the book. Typical of Newman, he put in a further caveat that he has some doubts as to the exactness of some of his minor facts.

It is not exactly clear why Newman wrote the novel, because it does not fall into the proposed pattern of titles of Wiseman's Catholic Library. There were some who thought he did it to show up the Cardinal but there is no real evidence for this. Certainly Newman as novelist is more appealing to a modern reader than is Wiseman, though neither would attract a wide reading public today. Newman's story may be more acceptable simply because his style is less dated. He is less inclined to exaggerate and to make his characters mere cardboard figures to act out his message. It must be said that *Callista* is less of a tract and more of a novel, while the same cannot be said for *Fabiola*.

When it was announced that Wiseman was writing a novel, his fellow cardinals were apparently somewhat perturbed, but when it appeared and was such a success they were full of approbation. Almost as if he were a neophyte author, Wiseman from the start took a very proprietary interest in this work, much more than he did with his more scholarly or theological efforts. He made arrangements with Henry Doyle for the illustrations, and when the initial sketches arrived he was quite careful to point out his disapprobation of artistic license. He did not much like Doyle's drawing of the Virgin, he wanted the inscriptions which were shown in the catacombs to be exact and he even noted that in one picture, 'The back of the chair is, I think, too high.' After further correspondence, the difficulties were resolved and the book printed to the Cardinal's satisfaction. The publishers were obviously optimistic about the book's being a success; the first printing was 4,000 copies.

Having made his debut in a new arena, Wiseman was the recipient of many letters of congratulation. Newman was most effusive and encouraged him to write a second volume. Wiseman toyed with the idea but did not write a sequel. Monsignor Talbot told him that the book had caused a sensation in Rome and that everyone was effusive in their praise. Typically, Pope Pius IX liked it and sent his congratulations, as did other prominent Catholic clerics and laymen. One significant Protestant, the King of Prussia, adored the book and said so; apparently he stayed up all one night to complete the reading of it.

What was the reaction of the professional critics? A perusal of such periodicals as *The Quarterly Review, The Edinburgh Review, Fraser's Magazine* and the like will show that *Fabiola* was not reviewed at all. Apparently the literary world considered Wiseman's effort either too slight for serious consideration, or too Roman Catholic in bias and orientation for the general reader. Indeed, even the *Dublin Review* only noticed it after it had been made into a play by Frederick Oakley, entitled *The Youthful Martyrs of Rome*, and it was reviewed in tandem with Newman's *Callista*. Oakley's version is mainly the vehicle for what might have been an ordinary review of Wiseman's work, but since the cardinal was one of the editors it was somewhat difficult to include his own efforts. The reviewer in the *Dublin Review* was aware of the problems confronting the author who attempts 'sacred fiction'. He observed that 'The great value of *Fabiola* . . . consists in the vividness, the completeness, and the truth of the picture which it presents of the early Christian life. What the Waverley Novels and their imitators have done for modern and mediaeval history, *Fabiola* has done with the most perfect success of the early Church; nor is there a topic in ecclesiastical archaeology, doctrinal, disciplinary, liturgical, asetic, ritual, or domestic, which is not fully illustrated in its pages, and illustrated without the slightest trace of pedantry or affectation of learning.' It should be added that the comments on *Callista* are equally commendatory.

The book had a complimentary press in popular Roman Catholic organs in Great Britain. Two editions of *Fabiola* were sold out in the first year. In the United States the book had equally popular success and two editions appeared in rapid succession. Oakley's poetic drama appeared in 1856 and another dramatic version by M. Soullier was published in 1867. Editions appeared in German, Italian, French, Spanish, Hungarian and even Danish and Dutch very soon after the initial publication. *Fabiola's* fame spread to South America where an edition was published in Bogota, Columbia, in 1865. It is probably one of the few books by a contemporary European author printed in that countrp at that time.

Even after Wiseman's death, editions continued to appear. In England new printings took place in 1896, 1904 and 1906. There was a Russian version in 1886, a new French edition in 1891, and a second one for schools in 1935; a Romansch edition in 1897, and one in Esperanto in 1911! In America its popularity did not die; new printings took place in 1874, 1886, 1896 and even in 1932 when a school edition was printed. In 1939 an edition appeared in Irish.[1]

Certainly few novelists at any time have had such a success. *Fabiola* was a real best-seller. Indeed, as a 'Sunday book', (one of those highly moral literary endeavours approved by pious parents for their children in the last century) it was almost a *beau-ideal* example. It contained nothing to shock, and was properly pious; even its Catholic theology was not excessive, and any but very Calvinistic or Evangelical households could accept its viewpoint. It had enough excitement to hold the attention of the reader and as Victorian literature gradually descended to the schoolroom, both boys and girls could find the story entertaining even if they did not comprehend all of the historical or theological points. To-day, it is unlikely that even the very young could take it seriously: the style would seem too archaic and the pace too slow. This is the fate which has befallen other novelists of the period, such as Charles Kingsley, Charlotte M. Yonge and Mrs. Craik. *Hypatia, A Dove in an Eagle's Nest* and *John Halifax, Gentleman*, now repose on library shelves or appear in those odd boxes of books which no one seems to buy. However, if one wished to understand an aspect of the last century, a perusal of them would be illuminating. The Victorians wanted their piety but they wanted it to be accompanied by action, or what they deemed to be action, and Wiseman's novel *Fabiola* aptly served both functions in more than an adequate mode.

Nicholas Wiseman's aims were modest. He wanted to demonstrate that good Roman Catholic fiction could be written and that it could find an enthusiastic audience. While we may question whether *Fabiola* is a good novel in the sense of a work of art, there is no doubt that the contemporary reading public responded generously. The author's sentiments about his book and how he saw what he had done might be summed up in a poem which he inscribed in a copy of *Fabiola* in 1860. Parenthetically, it should be observed that even here he could not abstain from those explanatory notes which had appeared in the novel itself.

Written in *Fabiola* at Monteporzio:

TO THE ENGLISH STUDENTS[2]

I

The thoughts, which in this book have taken form,
Are but reflections of things growing near;
As in sweet Nemi's mirror, soft and warm
Of Grail, church, tree, twin images appear;
Which if erased, or blurred, by ruffling storm,
Again, through innate art, glow new and clear.
So youth's impressions life's rough times deface;
Yet they resume, in calmer days, their shape and grace.

II

If not to you who read, to him who wrote,
These thoughts are flowers, bearing each its tale
Crushed in the page where youth has made its note,
'This rose I plucked in the Nomenton Vale;' [1]
'This palm-leaf where the shafts Sebastian smote;' [2]
'The Aurelian gave this bud, if young not frail.' [3]
They live again, though dry for many a year,
Sunned by a smile, or sometimes watered by a tear.

III

Then let Rome's light and shade, upon your breasts,
Leave its sun-picture; somewhat if it fade.
A word, a line, an hour of thoughtful rest
Will once more make it what your glance once made;
Well till Rome's fruitful earth, your toil be blest!
But spurn no flower, nor bruise beneath the spade;
For this is Rome's just gift — from sky to sod,
Sunbeam, or frogrance, binds us close to her and God.

Monteporzio, 27 March, 1860

NOTES ON THE POEM

[1]Where the Basilica of St. Agnes stands.
[2]The chapel marking this spot is almost overshadowed by a splendid palm, in the garden of St. Bonaventura.
[3]The church of St. Pancratius is situated on the road bearing this name.

5

Clio and the Cardinal

The votaries of Clio in the first half of the last century, as in this present century, were both amateurs and professionals, but at that time the line of demarcation between the two would often be hard to define, for the writing and studying of history was still very much part of a gentleman's education. Since it was not unusual for individuals in the intellectual world to write on historical subjects, it is somewhat surprising that Wiseman wrote so little that can be properly called historical. Both his *Horae Syriacae* and his essay on the *First Epistle of John* use historical evidence to support their basic arguments but cannot be deemed to be history in any modern sense of the idea.

Wiseman did not shun the writing of history *per se* but he had no inclination to do research as such, for he lacked the necessary patience and concern for detail which is the essence of the historian's craft. He used history for his own purposes, and while certainly never admitting it, he was very much with the eighteenth century and with Bolingbroke in particular in his assumption that history was philosophy, teaching by examples.

Many of his published lectures and pamphlets on a variety of subjects contain historical detail. For example, in his famous *Appeal to the Reason and Good Feeling of the English People in the Subject of the Catholic Hierarchy* which appeared in 1850 in the midst of the 'No Popery' crisis, he makes a number of historical allusions and remarks to buttress his main contention that the establishment of the hierarchy did not materially alter the situation. History was his servant and the historical material was evidence in his own course. He alludes to the past on all manner of occasions but does so as a polemicist and not as a scholar.

When Wiseman undertook to write an historical essay of sorts, it generally appeared in the *Dublin Review*. However, a number of other fugitive pieces appeared in other journals such as the *Catholic Magazine*. An example of this is an article which he wrote in 1837 entitled 'Early Italian Academies.' The article was really a review of two books, one by M. G. Libri and the other by Gay-Lussac. Wiseman's essay was written to refute the contention advanced by these authors, that the Roman Catholic Church was opposed to science. To support his position, he argued that it was incorrect to say, as had been implied by some scholars, that the Academia del Cemento at Florence was closed by Pope Clement XI in return for giving Leopoldo de Medici a red hat. Wiseman stated that the Academia simply expired because its chief patron was occupied with fresh interests and because its principal members went elsewhere. Wiseman denied that the Academia's members were tortured or otherwise maltreated, and he provided what he considered to be equally valid sources to support his arguments. He observed that this and similar bodies were not the objects of opposition by ecclesiastical authorities, but that their demise was occasioned by indifference. Wiseman was very conscious of the fact that the public, especially in non-Roman Catholic countries, had a fixed idea that the Church condemned all forms of scientific investigation. He maintained on a number of occasions that history does not prove the claim that the papacy deliberately censured scientific knowledge. While he would agree that heretical thought was condemned, science as such was not. He summoned Clio to assist in the presentation of what he deemed to be historical truth.

Another example of Wiseman's historical writings can be seen in his article entitled 'Boniface VIII' which appeared in the *Dublin Review* in November 1841,[1] and which was in fact a review of Sismondi's *History of the Italian Republics*. To gain the sympathy of his reader, Wiseman began his article by reflecting that historical judgment is not immutable. He went on to observe that antipathy towards the papacy was almost universal in protestant writings of the past but notes that in more recent times this is less true. His basic reason for this alteration of sentiment is a somewhat curious one. He observes that 'where he desired to assign a cause for this change in feelings and direction of historians, we should be inclined to attribute much to the noble character of recent pontiffs, whose lives broke down much prejudice against their order; not because they were better or wiser than their predecessors, but because the guidance of divine Providence brought forward their characters more prominently before the face of Europe than theirs who had preceded them.'[2] Presumably God has opened the eyes of many erstwhile critics and hence the papacy is seen in its true prespective, namely, as the leader against tyranny. To illustrate this he argues that Pius VII, the prisoner of Napoleon, was as much the victim as the ordinary man, and the former's Christian patience and exemplary character brought a new image to his office. Thereafter, even the most convinced Protestant could not fail to be affected and write in a more sympathetic fashion but in fact while historians were now less harsh perhaps in their treatment of the papacy it was not because the latter had necessarily improved in their opinion

110

but that it was rather less significant. Wiseman failed to appreciate that his contemporaries were less interested in popes because they were less interested in the church. Moreover, he was unable to comprehend that a 'good' pope such as Pius VII did not have the effect of changing scholarly attitudes to popes in general. Wiseman did not understand that the old shibboleths of 'good' and 'bad' were sufficient basis for judgment; to him the muse of history should use the same basis for moral attitudes as he did himself. He never hesitated to attribute the interpretations of scholars of his own day to more recent events and he equated the conflict between secular and religious authorities in the age of the enlightened despot with those of the middle ages. History may be philosophy teaching by examples as Bolingbroke says, but few of Wiseman's contemporaries would proceed to the extremes which he himself adopted.

Wiseman was not unaware that relatively few English Catholic scholars had been prepared to re-assess the historical past, but he never appeared to have asked himself why this should be. Was it that brilliant scholars were unwilling to risk attacks on their faith by secular-minded critics, or were there really too few intellectually competent persons who were convinced that there was a real need for historical revisionism? Certainly, experience would indicate that ecclesiastical authority in general—and this despite Wiseman's view that the Roman Catholic Church was open-minded — did not really welcome close examination. Too often in the past historical scholarship had been used as a weapon against religion, and such risks were not worth taking. For the majority of the leaders of the Church, ideas were suspect, for they could be the route to heresy. Simple faith sufficed and this, applied to academic writing, would result in right history. The consequence was that much Roman Catholic historiography was beneath scholarly contempt and even when it was not, it was bordering on hagiography.

Yet his attempted method of rehabilitation of Boniface VIII is illuminating for it illustrates how he saw the historian's function. He proceeds initially to take the viewpoint that Boniface was involved in a struggle of *'regale* and *pontificale'* like Pius VI or Pius VII. Having made his subject relevant, he then enquired whether the facts about Boniface were purely calumnious or were actually true. As a good scholar, he goes at once to contemporary or near contemporary writers, many of whom — such as Dante — are distinctly antipathetic; but then he very quickly dismisses them all and provides alternative arguments and alternative sources, not always germane, to refute their arguments.

Behaving rather like a lawyer defending a client, he considers each charge made against Boniface by scholars. He starts with the

111

claim that Boniface virtually forced his somewhat simple predecessor, Celestine V, to resign. Boniface had been accused of attempting to persuade Celestine to give up the papacy almost as soon as he was elected. To refute this, he then produces several authorities, contemporary with the events, to deny this charge. Not content with this, Wiseman goes further and even implies that Boniface tried to persuade his predecessor to remain as Pope; but such ardent partisanship is unnecessary since no less a person than Petrarch took the view that Celestine acted on his own responsibility. Having presented *his* evidence, Wiseman assumes it is obvious that his conclusions must be the correct ones, and that no other interpretations are possible.

Sismondi and other writers had attributed Pope Boniface's rise to power to fraud and chicanery. In reply, Wiseman asks how Boniface could have been elected unanimously if the College of Cardinals had not supported him. Moreover, Pope Celestine had created twelve new cardinals, seven of them French and none specifically Roman who might have supported Boniface, and it seems impossible to imagine that the latter could have bribed them all and even less likely that they would have allowed themselves to promote one who was so directly against their interests. Boniface was a Roman, and as such he would follow a course of action to diminish the influence of the foreign cardinals. Wiseman argues that Boniface's origins and previous career were well known and that his own contemporaries must have realized what their actions would do.

Thus, he sees the question in a larger context; he contends that the historians have made up their minds, regardless of the evidence, to see Boniface as an evil and wicked man. Wiseman believes that the evidence will not support such a sweeping generalization and is desirous of redressing the balance.

Boniface is only treated with some justice following his arrest by the French at Anagni. Almost everyone seems to agree that on this occasion he behaved with great dignity. To Wiseman this indicates that there were aspects of Boniface's character that historians generally refused to see because they did not wish to do so. He shows that even Dante in his *Purgatorio* is generous — the only time that he is — in Canto XX, lines 86-90. The historian Sismondi, a critic of Boniface, declines to see any good in the Pope; he has him go mad, chew his stick, and behave as a wild man. This story is completely false, says Wiseman, for Muratori, whom he cites as a source, actually denies the tale. Wiseman sees this as a further indication of Sismondi's duplicity and the rightness in his own historical view of Boniface.

Wiseman uses his material in a highly selective fashion and his facts are often as dubious as those which he wishes to refute; he is really more interested, to prove a case, in not giving the whole picture. He is not a historian at all as we would understand the term, but rather he is part of what is now, officially at least, a totally discredited tradition.

In a less quixotic and hagiographic tradition is Wiseman's history of concordats which appeared in a series of lectures delivered in 1855. He had decided that the British public simply was ignorant on the true nature of the subject, as it had been on the whole question of the hierarchy a few years earlier. He believed that the difficulties arose 'from a simple misunderstanding of the true state of the case . . .'[3] and the concern showed by the British over the Austro-papal agreement that had recently been signed came from the same root cause. Wiseman felt that the British excitement and alarm came in part from religious prejudice and in part from lack of knowledge. He noted that this concordat was 'made the subject of observation — not only has it been reproduced in various journals, and commented upon — not only have letters been written drawing from it the most extraordinary inferences, but it has been made the motive and the occasion of a series of writings exceedingly painful not alone to Catholics, who must keenly feel the bitterness and falsehood of the remarks made, but to everyone who has generous feeling, or who has at heart the real happiness and interests of his country.'[4] To dispel the confusion he believed it his duty to give the facts and to demonstrate that the English should have no apprehensions on what neither concerned them nor affected their interests. Although not always perceptive in understanding his fellow-countrymen, he was shrewd enough to recognize that the protestant element in society disapproved of the concordat between Emperor Francis Joseph and Pius IX largely because it restored to the papacy powers which it had earlier lost. The English liked the former state of affairs which seemed to represent an essentially protestant spirit.

To comprehend the essential nature of a concordat, Wiseman refers to St. Paul's *Epistle to the Romans*, Chapter 13: 'Render unto Caesar the things that are Caesar's, and unto God the things that are God's.' To ensure that both the secular and ecclesiastical authorities comprehended the limitations of their sovereignty it was necessary to define the specific areas of responsibility — for each had its own liberties and its own obligations. To understand all these facets of church-state relations, formal agreements had to be made, and these were the historical bases of concordats. Moreover, the Church might grant special favours to the state and *vice versa*, but in each case they are concessions and not rights; for neither side had the authority to enhance or extend the boundaries so defined in the concordat. Wiseman made use of the idea that law defines lawful liberty, and asserted that a concordat is really only a declaration of legal rights. In other words he simply wished to show that concordats were far from mysterious.

In an easy and familiar style he gave a brief history of concordats, drawing his illustrations where possible from English history. As early as 689 King Ina of the West Saxons drew up a code confirming the Church in its lawful rights; King Alfred did likewise, as did William the Conqueror, by reaffirming the charters of King Edward the Confessor. Later King John with the Magna Carta declared 'that the Church of England shall be free.' In all of these and in other decrees the papal legate was involved; this involvement emphasized an agreement between sovereign powers. Having shown the historical nature of the concordat he next turned to examine the first formal concordat which was between Francis I and Leo X; this was a treaty of nineteen articles arranging relations between the sovereign and the Pope.

As an introduction to the question of the Austro-Papal agreement which had inspired his lectures, he began by giving a brief history of church-state relations in the Hapsburg dominions since the time of Emperor Joseph II. As part of his reform programme the Emperor had arrogated to himself many powers which previously had been ecclesiastical. In this process, Wiseman thought the Church had lost its liberties, and although it was not alone in being 'reformed', he notes that 'it was the Church that Principally felt his [Emperor Joseph II's] power.' Wiseman believed, because he wanted to believe it, that the Josephine policies were generally unpopular. He seemed to think that the Emperor had it in mind to push towards a Henrican system and break entirely with Rome. After Joseph's death, his successor continued his policy but on the latter's death in 1789 a change resulted because Emperor Francis was more conservative and his policies were moderate, with the result that the Church supported the Emperor against Napoleon. Wiseman thought that history teaches that the true alliance of Church and state is the best protector of liberty against tyranny from within or without.

Although the Josephine legislation had been moderated, no real change occurred officially even after 1814 but this he does not seem to have understood, and he writes as if Metternich, whom he calls 'the faithful minister' and the 'illustrious statesman', had abrogated the Josephine legislation. Although Wiseman did not realize it, Metternich was a true son of the eighteenth century and favoured a strong centralized and authoritarian monarchy sharing no powers.

Francis I presumably had his own reasons for not acting, although Wiseman categorically states that on his deathbed he made it 'his most sacred bequest' to his heir that the latter 'totally abrogate the whole of the Josephine laws.' Deathbed admonitions are useful since they relieve the conscience of the dying and throw the onus on members of the next generation who may or may not choose to act. In this instance he really has no explanation why they did not act. Emperor Ferdinand I, whom Wiseman calls 'a truly religious and most exemplary and virtuous man, [who] cared not for the pomps and snares of royalty,' [6] did not follow out his late father's admonitions. Presumably external forces prevented this, or could they have been Metternichian *realpolitik*?

However, the laws were finally repealed by Francis Joseph in 1850. Protestants claimed that Pope Pius IX had been 'alluring or inducing' the young monarch 'to humble himself at his feet, and had wrung from him this law.' But there is no evidence extant to support such an idea and Wiseman is quite correct to discard this line of argument because Pius IX was really in no position to induce anyone to humble himself, least of all Austria which with France had restored him to his position. The result of Francis Joseph's action was that the Empire had *no* specific church-state relations in a legal sense at all. Careful examination would indicate that Francis Joseph had really given nothing back to the Church, for the Josephine legislation had been inoperative for nearly half a century. While *de jure* it existed, *de facto* the Church and state were more or less sovereign in their own spheres.

To explain the nature of the agreement between Pius IX and Francis Joseph, Wiseman analyses the terms of the concordat in both their specific and their historic contexts. He pointed out, for example, that an episcopal officer — that is a bishop — takes an oath of fealty *before* his consecration — shades of Henry II and Becket — not to involve himself in any activities that would injure the state. Wiseman showed that this practice arose in the Middle Ages and he indicates in a series of notes how the admission of bulls from Rome was subject to royal scrutiny prior to their publication and that the clergy accepted this, thus fulfilling the oath not to act in any way that might injure the state. The origin of the *Statutes of Praemunire* and *Provisors* both arose from the duality of authority and the insistence of the sovereign to ensure that his rights were respected.

Referring anew to the agreement between Pius IX and Francis Joseph, he points out how the concordat retains the historic rights of the Hapsburgs in Hungary, that is, the right of nominating bishops. This is really not too unlike the powers possessed by the British Prime Minister and Wiseman hastened to point out the similarity. Moreover, the special privileges of the Apostolic King of Hungary — having the cross carried before him like an archbishop — and also his legatine authority, are all in the concordat.

Therefore, having drawn on historical examples, he felt that he had been able to illustrate that the concordat was not something dangerous to anyone, least of all to the English. In his lectures, he used history in a didactic sense. He produced evidence to underline a lesson, to illustrate a specific point of view. The philosophical conclusions existed from the beginning; the evidence merely illustrated the truth.[8]

The third kind of historical work written by Wiseman was somewhat different as it had no very high motives; he was not attempting to teach a lesson or restore a reputation. He himself describes his *Recollections of the Last Four Popes and of Rome in Their Times*:

> This is not a history, nor a series of biographies, not a journal, nor what are called memoirs. It is so much of a great moving picture as caught one person's eye, and remained fixed upon his memory: touched him most closely, interested more deeply his feelings. . . . And let this sincere account of one witness have its place among the materials of a future historian, who may, perhaps be searching for those, by preference, which proceed not from anonymous sources, or secondary evidences, but from such as write what they have seen with their eyes, heard with their ears, and touched with their hands, and who, at the risk of unpopularity, fear not to subscribe their depositions. It may be said, that a darker and shadier side must exist in every picture . . . much vice, corruption, misery, moral and physical, which form no part of our description. . . . Let the historian blend and combine the various and contrasting elements of truth telling witnesses. But to the author, such narratives would have been impossible.[9]

Wiseman here states his premises for the work. It is clear that *Recollections of the Last Four Popes* is not history in the modern sense nor in the accepted view of professional scholars of the last century. It is a sort of bowdlerized history, a very personal statement in that he only intends to report good things; he even avows that he 'does not retain in his memory histories of startling wickedness, nor pictures of peculiar degradation.'[10] As he is writing of his youthful experiences, the happy days in Rome, he romanticizes about the events and the people. Moreover, as his heroes are popes, he can only see them through the most rose-coloured of spectacles.

It must be noted that, from the start, Wiseman denied that he was writing biographies of the popes; yet he does make them the focal points of his narrative and moreover, he does write biographical essays — all carefully pruned and hagiographic. These essays are an essential part of the narrative, and everything is linked to the lives of the popes.

As for the sources for his volume, despite the denial that he had written a journal, it is clear that Wiseman had used a diary of sorts, and copies of correspondence; for it is highly unlikely that he could recollect in such detail all the facts as he does in quite so precise a manner. While the events recounted are often given in general enough terms, there are also reports of conversations and the like which simply could not have been remembered without some reference to notes taken at the time.

Why then is this book not a memoir in the traditional sense? Firstly, because the author denies it in his introduction; secondly, because although there are references to himself, they are always in the third person; (this could be construed as a stylistic affectation and one used later by Henry Adams for example, but Wiseman as Wiseman is not the central figure in the narrative in a specific fashion). Thirdly, Wiseman is not the 'hero' of his own narrative, which is customarily the case in memoirs; and finally, there are large sections of the book in which Wiseman *per se* does not appear at all, suggesting that the account could have been written by any observer of the scene.

The book is history, but only in the most special sense of the idea of history. An eminent nineteenth-century American historian, Justin Windsor, saw his work as a holding up of a mirror to catch the reflections. He too uses a similar metaphor and defines his work as a 'moving picture caught in one person's eye.' Thereby he is catching only certain images which peculiarly attract his attention; there are images deliberately excluded, or unnoticed.

Since there were relatively few books on the papacy available to the ordinary reader in the first half of the nineteenth century, the general theme of this book was of considerable interest. True, there were a number of works which were polemical in nature, generally strongly anti-Roman Catholic about the wickedness of Rome and the 'scarlet woman'; but there were few books that were informative and that had any real evidence of being accurate. For many Englishmen the Pope was the ally of Lucifer, but at the same time the city of Rome had attracted numerous British visitors, many of whom had seen the various Popes despite their supposed

117

satanic connections and had even been received by them. Even so, the visitors to Rome came only from a limited segment of society. Thus, when Wiseman undertook to write his enthusiastic book about four incumbents of the papal office, he was producing something that was rather unique.

He ingeniously combined his hagiography, for such were his biographical accounts, with travel literature which was extremely popular at the time; by writing in this way he could attract a class of reader who might otherwise have rejected the book entirely. His somewhat lush style and his own enthusiasm for Rome combined to make the opening chapter — his own arrival on the scene — very charming and appealing to his own generation.

Moreover, he was able to explain all sorts of customs, events and procedures from personal experience. The interior of the Quirinal and the Vatican palaces were closed to most people. What went on inside? How were persons received? Avid curiosity about the details of life in high places was no different in the past century from what it is today. Wiseman was able to write in a definitive fashion about life in very special places inhabited by very special sovereigns and princes.

His biographical sketches of Pius VII, Leo XII, Pius VIII and Gregory XVI are all written *con amore*. He could do this, not only from personal inclination but because he was aware that most of his readers knew nothing specific of these men or their backgrounds. Pius VII is summarized as being 'the mildest of men';[11] Leo XII 'was courteously bland and winning. . . .'[12] The favourite pursuit of Pius VIII, Wiseman wrote, was 'biblical literature,'[13] and he went on to describe Gregory XVI as a man in whom 'A peculiar simplicity of habits was remarkable.'[14] Since the internal workings of the Roman Catholic Church were *terra incognita*, he had here a topic that could not fail to command an interest. Recognizing his special position of authority, Wiseman recounted in detail a papal election (including all the fascinating facts on the famous veto cast by the monarchs of Spain, France and Austria), a papal coronation with its splendour (but with nice little asides like the thrice burning of the flax to symbolize the transience of the world's glory), and a papal funeral. There is also a very complete account of a jubilee year. Popes are all shown to be human, visiting the colleges, prisons and monasteries, and not the ogres they were popularly supposed to be. There are nice domestic details about the Pope's private life: what sort of meals they eat, and why there exists a tradition that Popes dine alone; which Popes received formally — for example, Pius VIII who received and gave audiences from his throne, thus making personal conversation difficult — and which Popes were more intimate and easy. The book is also filled with that sort of information which Frederick Rolfe later would have loved: 'Although it is a well-known fact that a Pope on his accession takes a new name, by usage one already in the catalogue of his predecessors, it is not generally known that, in the signature to the original of Bulls, he retains his original Christian name. Thus Leo XII would continue to sign himself as "Hannibal", and the present Pope [Pius IX] signs "John" at the foot of the most important ecclesiastical documents. The form is, "Placet Joannes." ' [15]

Another somewhat mysterious matter, that of cardinals being named *in petto*, is dealt with thoroughly: Wiseman points out that when the individual is publicly proclaimed, he actually takes the precedence he would have had if he had been named initially, but he does not explain the reason for this practice. He tells the story that Lammenais was actually named *in petto* by Leo XII but never proclaimed. Considering Lammenais' later career and ultimate excommunication, this is a not unamusing story. Wiseman uses it to refute the myth that Lingard was the man to whom Leo XII alluded in a Consistory as one 'of great talents, an accomplished scholar, whose writings, drawn *ex authenticis fontibus*, had not only rendered great service to religion, but had delighted and astonished Europe.' [16] Lammenais himself is later described: 'But in him there was long a centre deeply sunk. There was a maggot in the very core of that beautiful fruit. . . . [He had] the demon of pride and ambition.' [17]

Wiseman, knowing that his book was written for his fellow countrymen, gave a good deal of information on the English College — a few passing remarks are given on the Irish college too — on general relations with England, and on the question of the creation of English cardinals. The story of Bishop Baines is reported most tactfully. Baines, a Benedictine, was initially an obvious choice for a red hat, but his personality and his ideas were such that he could not be elevated. Wiseman's account of the elevation of Thomas Weld is just the sort of thing which would fascinate the Victorians. Weld was a member of the 'old Catholic' gentry, had married and had a daughter. After the latter's marriage to Lord Clifford's heir in 1818 — Weld himself was a widower by this time — he became a priest. He was named coadjutor to the Bishop Vicar-Apostolic of Upper Canada, then moved to Rome and finally in 1830 became a cardinal where he was to be the papal advisor in English matters. Curiously enough, during his years in Rome his daughter acted as his hostess. A second English cardinal was Charles Acton, an uncle of the great historian; Acton's early life was somewhat peculiar; he was partly educated at protestant schools such as Westminster and attended Magdalene College, Cambridge, long before the statutes of Cambridge University were changed to permit any but Anglicans to take their degrees. He became a cardinal at the age of 39 in 1842, five years after Weld's death. Following Acton's own demise in 1847, there were no Englishmen who were members of the College of Cardinals until Wiseman was named in 1850. These and other similar facts were related in an artless and simple manner.

No book on Rome of any sort would be complete without an account of art and archaeology. To illustrate that the Church was not the enemy of scholarship, he next discussed the various archaeological discoveries made with papal approval and the various collections of the Vatican. Each Pope is shown to be a true patron of the arts, generous and also knowledgeable. Wiseman had his own views on art criticism. Michelangelo was superb, a 'burst of individual genius, not to be imitated with impunity by any less than himself.' [18] Canova . . . 'revived, or raised from a low state of affectation, exaggeration, and meanness of conception . . . [and] his return to the simple beauty, the calm attitudes, the quiet folds, the breadth and majesty of ancient works, soon put him at the head of a European school.' [19] Thorwaldson, his successor, comes in for high praise too. Wiseman cared little either for baroque or for the artistic conventions in the decades after the French Revolution, saying that a 'cold classical school sprang up in Europe, of which David was the type in France, . . . which sought its subjects in an unclean mythology or a pagan heroism, and its forms in the motiveless and rigidly accurate markers of antique production.' [20]

Nevertheless, his history was not all merely a picture of life with the Popes. He knew that brigands had a Quixotic allure too. To him brigandage was the natural child of the revolution and French rule and it was ended by the just rule of the restored government as a result of the efficient activities of the well-organized Roman police and army. To show how wicked the brigands were, Wiseman tells the story of the kidnapping of the Camoldolese monks and of their rescue by the gallant soldiers. Brigandage was almost extinct by the end of Pius VII's reign, but it had revived anew because of the revolutionary spirit. 'The legitimate sovereign is held responsible for the evils resulting from rebellion against him; and they who write to stimulate revolution, use as an argument in its favour the necessity of repressing a mischief which revolution has engendered.' [21]

Wiseman's account of the revolution of 1830 is wildly romantic.

Gregory XVI had just been elected and there were reports of trouble in Modena, but as it was carnival time, nothing came of it. A plot to take Castel St. Angelo was thwarted and the attack on the post office was repelled by the brave soldiers. Private citizens barricaded their houses, and the colleges were put into a state of defence. The English College took 'every precaution against nocturnal surprise. . . . After a careful survey of the premises, only one weak point was discovered . . . and I doubt if Todleben himself could have suggested a more scientific or more effective way than we employed of securing it . . . against nocturnal aggression.' [22]

As Wiseman saw it, the citizens of the papal capital were opposed to the revolution, but he does admit that the provincials were not necessarily of like mind; to prove this, he notes that the Civic Guard was enlarged. 'Multitudes presented themselves for enrolment; and among these, persons of the highest class, eager to take on themselves the defence of the Pope's sacred person.' [23] The lower classes too were exceedingly loyal and 'they expressed their attachment and readiness to fight, with a clamour and warmth that would have rendered any attempt to remove them a dangerous experiment.' [24] The Pope, as befitted a noble man, remained calm; he was aware that the revolt had 'no personal nature, no enmity to himself. It rose against the rule, not against the ruler; against the throne, not against its actual possessor.' [25] To Wiseman, Pope Gregory was the man of virtue, fighting rascally radicals, nay worse, obvious republicans with the worst of motives and the lowest of ideals and activities. To rectify the situation foreign troops were called in, and the revolt put down. Gregory XVI as Wiseman would have us believe, now improved conditions in government, codified the law, created a national bank, improved the coinage and undertook vast public works. In sum, he did an heroic work and the papal states were bound to be happy, and in his terms they were. Other observers took a less sanguine viewpoint of the situation.

Like most of his contemporaries in Britain, Wiseman was decidedly Russophobic, and to illustrate his antipathy he tells of the interview between Tsar Nicholas I and Pope Gregory. At this point, relations between Rome and St. Petersburg were very bad and the whole question of the Roman Catholic Church in the Russian empire was the subject of the talks. This is Wiseman's description of the meeting:

> eagle, glossy, fiery, . . . in all the glory of pinions which no The imperial visitor entered with his usual firm and royal aspect, grand as it was from statue-like features, stately frame and martial bearing; free and at his ease, with gracious looks and condescending gestures of salutation . . . the Imperial

flight had ever wearied, of beak and talon which no prey had yet resisted. He came forth again, with head uncovered, and hair, if it can be said of man, dishevelled; haggard and pale, looking as though in an hour he had passed through the condensation of a protracted fever; taking long strides, with stooping shoulders, unobservant, unsaluting . . . and hurried away. . . . It was the eagle dragged from his eyrie among the clefts of the rocks . . . his feathers crumpled, and his eye quelled, by a power till then despised.[26]

Even the strongest anti-Roman Catholic Englishman could not have quarrelled with the Cardinal's unflattering account of Nicholas I.

As an historical work this is at best *petit histoire*. It is too sentimental and too romantic to be more than that because Wiseman sees all his heroes — and these are not only the incumbents of the See of St. Peter but their intimates as well, such as Cardinals Consalvi, Gustinioni and Mai — as men without flaws. Any enemy of the papacy, be he a political revolutionary or a theological critic, is damned without mercy. He really ought to have been able to write good history — he had the scholarly expertise and background — but he did not succeed, and his activities in the service of Clio were non-existent. It is a bit surprising that he failed to write anything that could be called history since he attempted almost every other form of literary endeavour. His style was not necessarily against him although it was often too lush and too involved to be thoroughly satisfying. Still, it is true that historians of the romantic school did write overblown prose. If Wiseman be an historian at all, it is only in the sense that he used history to support his own preconceptions. The material was very obviously manipulated, and the facts were selected, not without some real skill, to produce the result that he had already desired. His historical writings were either polemical, didactic or entertaining but were not necessarily true. Wiseman proves too much and hence proves nothing.

Recollections of the Last Four Popes was well enough received by the audience to which it was directed. It appealed to Wiseman's co-religionists and it was also read by those who wanted to know more about Rome but not in too serious a fashion. There were critics to be sure. One of the harshest of Wiseman's opponents was Alessandro Gorozzi who wrote a volume of about the same length in which he refuted almost everything which Wiseman had said. Gorozzi's book is as bad as Wiseman's in that his men of virtue are also too white and his men of evil too black; Garozzi is Wiseman inside out.

As noted previously, Wiseman did not have the temperament to write orthodox history, for he was too impetuous and too hurried. He was best at putting down his ideas just as they came to him. He was too indolent to use sources carefully and he was always too concerned with things of the moment to be able to have the necessary detachment so essential for proper scholarly activities. Nevertheless, he could write real history if he chose; for example, a 'Brief Account of the Council Held at Constantinople AD 1166,' appeared in *The Catholic Magazine* in 1833. This short piece was not polemical and it was a piece of good expository writing on an historical subject. It demonstrated that Wiseman knew how to use sources, how to be critical; but this was in his youth, long before all the controversies and difficulties beset him. Later, he can only be said to have been an enthusiast, not a scholar. Perhaps a fellow Roman Catholic commenting on the *Recollections* summed it up best: 'It is a tribute of grateful affection from one on whom each Pontiff conferred many favours. It is a pleasing, a popular and in many respects a valuable book.' However, he did not say that it was history.

In his early days Wiseman published *Lectures on Science and Revealed Religion*, the text of lectures he had delivered in Rome. At first glance it would seem difficult to categorize such a book as history, and, indeed, it is doubtful if Wiseman personally would have done so. It is not history as Wiseman's own contemporaries would have conceived it, for the book does not concentrate on past politics, the doings and undoings of kings and queens, wars and treaties. It is rather an elaboration of certain cultural — in the broadest sense — traditions which combine to form the basis of western thought; as such it is history in the very best sense. Although not construed as historical writing, it must be seen as such.

Wiseman's aim in this work was to demonstrate that revealed religion and science as it was then understood were not incompatible, and he utilized the writings of his own scientific contemporaries to provide him with the evidence to support his theories. This scientific information was supported by the writings of German philosophers such as Schlegel and Fichte and he added to these other scholarly treatises of an historical and anthropological nature. As with most of Wiseman's writings, these lectures were popular in that they were not directed to a scholarly audience. Rather, they were designed for a literate audience, initially for his own pupils and later for the general public. The aims of the lectures were once again frankly didactic.

In his efforts to support his contentions that science and religion were not incompatible and that one revealed the truth of the other, Wiseman decided against the use of the traditional philosophical methods to promote his case but chose rather a more novel one, that of applying a sort of cultural anthropology in what he deemed to be an historical way to demonstrate the truth of the Christian message and the Bible.

He does not begin in an easy fashion but concentrates initially on the study of historical linguistics — hardly a simple introduction to his topic — by comparing the various linguistic traditions; he makes lists of common words and, with evidence from Schlegel and Herder among others, he arrives at the conclusion that once there was one language. He then proceeds to take the 'leap of faith' and asserts that the books of Moses must be true since our common ancestor was Adam and he and his wife spoke one language. It was only later, after the flood and the tower of Babel, that God dispersed mankind and gave to each of the groupings special intellectual attributes as seen in their development of speech and words; this is not a very satisfying explanation certainly, and appears decidedly simplistic.

After satisfying himself on the unity of language, Wiseman moved on to consider the natural history of man, basing many of his interpretations on the differing ethnic origins of man and animal on the nature of environment. He accepts without question that the animal world changes when given a change of its surroundings, a sort of Lysenkoesque viewpoint, and cites as evidence the case of European dogs which, according to report, degenerated on the Gold Coast and became very much like the native wild animals already there. As a sort of extra form of scientific evidence he asserts that by the features of man, one can tell those to whom some degree of civilization and culture is possible. This is phrenology basen on physiognomy. He uses for his example the people of Ethiopia and the inhabitants of North Africa, both having a religion with a professed revelation, Christian and Islamic; Wiseman sees this as a sign of a higher civilization—while those without this are the Africans who are believers in fetishism and idolatry and are at the lowest cultural level. He supported these rather idiotic views by asserting that in America the field hand retains more of the features and cultural characteristics of the original African than does the house servant. (Does he not think that miscegenation might have something to do with it?) What he is saying, and here he was far from unique, is that the physical features of men show their degree of civilization. He totally rejected the idea of the descent of man from animals, and he vigorously opposed a French scholar who claimed that the Hottentot in Africa was related to the baboon. He goes further in denying Lamarck's *Philosophie Zoologique* with ith gradation of animals (Darwin was to elaborate on all of this later) and its statement that acquired characteristics brought animals and ultimately man into the state of physical being as he now is. Wiseman simply says Lamarck is wrong; history as seen proves it and scripture supports what is observable.

Having dismissed Lamarck and like-minded scientists, he attempted to show that geology supported the Mosaic story. From the evidence found by geologists, the date of creation seems to be supported by scientific writing. What Wiseman does it to use the known facts of pre-history and geological science to write an early history of man. He is pleased, but perhaps hardly surprised, to discover that his historical-cum-scientific writings concur in the main with the Old Testament, but he fails to state that in presenting his viewpoint, he has chosen his material carefully. Of course, he would be highly indignant if he were accused of selecting evidence to support a preconceived position and one which, as a convinced orthodox Roman Catholic, he was bound to believe. His response to such a charge would be that his work was supported by the best authorities and simply supported the historical position adopted by the Church. Thus the Christian cosmography, while in itself true, was demonstrated to be so to skeptics by evidence which the skeptical could not fail to accept.

In this study of science and religion Wiseman includes three chapters which were real history in a traditional sense, and this was one of the few occasions in his entire career when he did so. These three chapters are all concerned with early history, not necessarily that of Western Europe but *l'histoire universale*, with considerable emphasis on the oriental world. He is not uncritical in his treatment of the subject and observes sagely: 'In Nature . . . there is no pride, no desire, and no power to represent herself other than in reality she is. But if we ask the oldest nations when they sprang up, and when they first entered on the career of their social existence, there arise instantly, in the way of a candid reply, a multitude of petty ambitions, jealousies and prejudices; and there intervenes between us and the truth a mist of ignorance, wilful or traditional, which involves the inquiry both in mystery and perplexity, and leaves us to find our way by the aid of the most uncertain elements, with the constant danger of most serious error.' [27]

While he recognized that historians in the past had embellished their stories with very dubious factual evidence, modern historians rejected such arts, and in their search for truth had developed new techniques. However, in the process the charm of much that passed for history was lost.

Wiseman was a great believer in the significance of artefacts for he was convinced that archaeological remains were directly supportive of the written evidence. This may not be very original, but Wiseman thought that physical remains often gave a direct allusion to written historical facts, particularly to those which often seem unnatural or obscure. To be sure, artefacts do give some support to biblical stories but it may be somewhat extreme to say 'that archaeology . . . while it enlightens and delights us, may well form the basis of the strongest religious impressions and individual evidences.'

Moving somewhat abruptly from archaeology and historical anthropology, Wiseman applies some of his general views on history to what he calls 'oriental studies' and 'oriental literature' which to him means biblical scholarship. He was certain that literary studies, particularly *explication de texte*, could illuminate the historical process. The literature of a society gave him a real explanation of certain social and ideological aspects which appeared less clear in the more traditional historical sources.

Although he was technically discussing science and religion and the sources of conflict, in fact Wiseman was writing a form of *Kultur geschichte*. He writes about classical antiquity, Indian astronomy, Roman history, biblical scholarship and even Lamaism in Tibet, to say nothing of the historical and philosophical basis for scientific development of thought. In sum, in many ways his historical writings are very much in the eighteenth-century tradition which e would seem to abhor. He either produces *petit histoire* or *histoire universale*, both popular products of authors in the century before his own time. However, his aims were totally unlike those of the enlightenment. He believed that all knowledge correctly studied would illuminate the truth of the Christian religion. The scholar must 'go on, ever striving to approach nearer and nearer the attainment of a perfect representation [i.e. truth]. . . . Those that come after us will, peradventure, smile at the small comprehensions granted to our age, of nature and her operations: we must be content, amidst our imperfect knowledge, with having striven after that which is more full.' Even Voltaire could not quarrel with such lofty aims and what modern scholar could do more?

6

The Review and the Reviewer

Nearly a hundred years after Wiseman's death, the editorial board of the *Dublin Review*, which had been founded in 1835, decided to alter the name to the *Wiseman Review* with the Cardinal's coat of arms gracing the cover. The reasons for making the change were basically twofold; firstly, because of Nicholas Wiseman's long personal association with the journal and, secondly, because the editors wished to end the somewhat mistaken impression that it was largely concerned with Irish affairs. Perhaps this decision of the editorial board may be construed as the final accolade given to Wiseman for his intellectual and literary endeavours. While he was essentially a modest man, there is little doubt that he would have been pleased and all the more so to have 'his' review still continue in the tradition which he and the co-founders had originally envisaged.

As a result of Catholic Emancipation in 1829, Roman Catholics were now legally able to disseminate their ideas and their philosophy to a wider public. One of the consequences of this was the foundation of the *Dublin Review*; while numerous tracts and pamphlets were published to expound upon special issues and topics, it was really the periodical which provided the regular means for the expression of ideas on a variety of subjects of current interest. Early in the nineteenth century the Whigs had established *The Edinburgh Review* whose success was such that the Tories followed suit a few years later with *The Quarterly Review*. These journals attracted the best minds of the day with respect both to leadership and authorship. Macaulay and Brougham, for example, wrote for *The Edinburgh Review* while Sir Walter Scott and Southey were to do the same thing for *The Quarterly Review*. Although the articles were unsigned, the calibre of the literary talent was obvious and the authors were given an ample opportunity to express their opinions on literary, political and social matters. Moreover, by writing for a regular periodical, the writers were able to reach a rather wider public than might well have been the case had their material only been published in a pamphlet or in a book. The fact that the articles were all unsigned permitted an even freer expression of opinion than might otherwise have been the case. The obvious influence of *The Edinburgh Review* and *The*

Quarterly Review caused others to found similar periodicals such as the Benthamite *The Westminster Review* which had a decidedly utilitarian viewpoint, as also did *The Saturday Review* with authors such as J. A. Froude and James Bryce.

The Roman Catholics already had a periodical called *The Catholic Magazine*, which largely reflected the opinions of the old Catholic community and consequently was somewhat conservative in its outlook. To Wiseman and others who shared his views, *The Catholic Magazine* was very parochial and failed to appreciate the wider aspects of the church. While he wrote for the journal he was unsatisfied with the general editorial policy because he wanted a periodical to reflect an activist Roman Catholic ideology and theology. Wiseman believed that *The Catholic Magazine* was insufficiently 'Roman' and hence not truly part of the ecumenical character of the Church.

The *Dublin Review* came into being in December 1835. It had its origins in part in Wiseman's sermons and lectures in the autumn of the same year. Because he had been so successful and his lectures had received such commendation, Daniel O'Connell approached him to solicit help in founding a periodical reflecting the best of Roman Catholic ideas and writings. Wiseman, who had seen the need for such a review for some time, was most enthusiastic and agreed to become one of the editors, holding the position until his death. Prior to his acceptance of editorial duties he did put one limitation on policy; knowing as he did of O'Connell's political activities, he insisted 'that no extreme political views should be introduced into the Review.'[1] Wiseman saw his own rôle in simple terms; he was 'to represent the theological and religious elements in the journal,' while his colleagues on the board, Daniel O'Connell and M. J. Quin were to deal with the secular aspects of the quarterly. The new periodical was to be called the *Dublin Review* and Wiseman observed that it should 'belong to the present day: that is, should treat of living questions . . . [and] should grapple with real antagonists.'[2]

While there was no formal statement of policy in the first number which appeared in May 1836, Wiseman himself wrote to a correspondent concerning the aims of the *Dublin Review* as follows: 'It seemed the favourable moment to strike a chord, and stir up a spirit yet slumbering, but ready to awake. The Catholic religion as she is in the fulness of her growth, with the grandeur of her ritual, the beauty of her devotions, the variety of her institutions, required to be made known to many.'[3] His own contribution to the first issue was a long article entitled 'The Oxford Controversy' which surveyed the literature on the so-called 'Hampden Controversy'.

The controversy had arisen following Hampden's appointment as Regius Professor of Divinity at Oxford because Hampden's theological position was suspect in the eyes of many Anglicans. In the second number of the *Review*, which appeared in the following July, Wiseman wrote on the philosophy of art and on the state of religion in Italy. None of his pieces were short — they averaged eight thousand words — and were to be typical of his numerous writings in the *Dublin Review* over the years.[4]

He was very anxious for the new review to be a success; he wanted it to be read not only by Roman Catholics but also by intelligent people of all denominations. He never intended that it should be a theological magazine but rather an intellectual and sophisticated periodical not unlike the other reviews and differing from them only in that the general philosophy was Roman Catholic rather than protestant or political. So concerned was he for the success of the new venture that he postponed his return to Rome until the second number had actually appeared in print. For the next four years he continued to reside in Rome and to be Rector of the English College but at the same time he was to be actively involved with the review. In the first ten numbers he had an article in almost every issue and he selected the contributions by other writers as well.

If one surveys the numerous articles written by Wiseman from 1836 until his death nearly thirty years later, the general breakdown is as follows: 50 per cent theology, 20 per cent miscellaneous (this includes politics and science), 5 per cent travel, 10 per cent literature, 10 per cent art and 5 per cent history. Because of his own very real and continued interest in the Oxford Movement and the writings of its proponents and opponents, it was natural that articles on this subject should command much of his attention. *Tracts for the Times* were discussed in extended articles in 1837 and again in 1838, while *Froude's Remains*, a series of pieces written by Hurrell Froude, was the basis for another article in 1839. His own Church, too, provided similar themes. Roman Catholic theology and doctrine were considered extensively in the early years of the *Dublin Review* in pieces by Wiseman, with articles on such subjects as the Catholic versions of the scripture or on the authority of Rome in South America.

While Wiseman was himself an enthusiastic reader of travel literature, he seems to have allowed others to write on this genre and even when he did review travel books, he seems to have selected rather second-rate works and his own articles are rather feeble. As a matter of personal choice, he preferred to write articles and reviews on travel literature concerned only with Italy and

Rome. He obviously preferred the authors who saw Italy as he did, that is, authors who were respectful and adoring. However, he did not entirely limit himself, and in 1842 he reviewed Mrs. Trollope's *A Visit to Italy* — combining it with Charles Dickens' *American Notes* — but his title for this article, which appeared early in 1843, was 'Superficial Travelling' which clearly indicates his general sentiments. Both Mrs. Trollope and Dickens had prejudices which he found distasteful, and while he was not unperceptive in his comments on these authors, his own innate bias was all too evident. This was not untypical of him as an author. He could be remarkably balanced in his consideration of larger intellectual and theological questions but upon lesser matters he was frequently rather bigoted.

Considering his great personal interest in history, it is surprising that Wiseman did not actually write more on the subject, and he seems to have almost consciously refrained from reviewing most of the famous historical writings of his own day. With the rise of the Whig school and its commentary on English and Irish history, it is curious that he did not use their published work as a vehicle for expressing his own ideas on the subject. In fact, most of his historical reviews are concerned with classical antiquity or mediaeval history and again more with Italy than elsewhere. His failure to write articles on historical subjects is regrettable since he was at his best in controversial writings and much of the historical scholarship of his own day — particularly in the first decade of the review — would have been almost an obvious choice for his consideration since it was so decidedly against his own ideas on the subject. To be sure, historical literature was not neglected in the *Dublin Review*, but the pieces were contributed by the other authors.

His miscellaneous reviews include some very curious items. He wrote a most engaging piece on Sir Francis Head's volume *The Emmigrant* in 1847. This book, a re-writing of some of Head's writings on his own experience in North America, is treated most kindly. What is more surprising perhaps is that Wiseman did not review Head's volume, *A Fortnight in Ireland*, which was very hostile to the Roman Catholics. Indeed, it should be noted that Wiseman wrote little about Ireland; it may well be that his association with O'Connell and his own deliberately avowed policy of eschewing 'extreme political views' prevented him from doing so. Moreover, Ireland was certainly too controversial a subject for a Roman Catholic cleric of some eminence to consider if he wished to retain a credibility with his readers. As well, he was long associated politically with the Whigs and he might well have found the subject embarrassing. It was not until late in his life that he left the Whigs and became a supporter of the Tories, but at that time Ireland was less immediately politically significant. Even so, the switch in his political allegiance did not encourage him to write on Irish problems.

Much of the general literature upon which he chose to comment was puerile and jejeune in the extreme. His little account of the Sobieski Stuart volume *Tales of the Century* in January 1847 is too slight to be worthy of real consideration. It is instructive to observe, however, that such romantic literature caught his fancy enough to encourage him to do a piece of two thousand words. More significant as literature was Newman's novel — then published anonymously — *Loss and Gain* which was the basis for a long article. Wiseman, well aware who had written the book, praised it highly and commended it to his readers. It has been suggested that Newman's success as a novelist inspired Wiseman himself to enter the field of fiction for it was only a few years later that his own novel *Fabiola* — a very different sort of work to be sure — was written.

Wiseman had considerable fondness for a now forgotten writer named Catherine Sinclair. Three of her works received extended treatment by him. Two of her novels, *Beatrice* — a good three decker—and *London Homes*, also in three volumes, were discussed in 1853 and used as the basis for comment on the general treatment of Roman Catholics in literature. Another work by the same author entitled *Popish Legends or Bible Truths*, was the subject of an article called 'Lady Theologians', but in this instance Wiseman was at one with Johnson on the subject of women preachers. Since Wiseman was such a well-read man personally, it is astounding to think that he could devote himself to such trivia. Of course, it must be recognized that often the books in question were merely the basis for an article, but even so he could have served the same purpose with works of more intellectual and literary significance. All this may indicate that Wiseman was not particularly profound in his thinking and that, while intelligent, was not very original.

Certainly some very varied books which passed through his hands were selected as the basis for articles. He took up Henry Mayhew's *London Labour and London Poor* in the summer of 1851 and made it the basis for a most perceptive article on poverty. A rather different work, and somewhat more exotic, was Andrea de Torio's *Gestures of the Ancients Sought in the Gesticulations of the Neapolitans*. This curious volume provides the basis for an article of fifteen pages; Wiseman used it to explain to the Anglo-Saxon world some of the characteristics of Latin society. An article on advertising, not entirely complimentary, arose from Wiseman's reading of *The Supplement to the Times* in 1851. A similar sort of publication, the catalogue of the exhibition of the Royal Academy for 1847, was conjoined to Lord Lindsay's *Sketches of the History of Christian Art* for one of his many articles on art.

Wiseman was naturally conservative when it came to dealing with Italian politics. In the late 1840's and thereafter, a number of articles appeared supporting papal policy. Throughout all of them it is evident that Wiseman was opposed unalterably to any change in the political state in Italy. Volumes such as Montalembert's *Pius IX and Lord Palmerston,* Ierson's *Rome and European Liberty,* and Bowyer's *Lombardy, the Pope and Austria* all provided the basis for criticism of liberal attempts to promote Italian unity, and destroy the papal states. Indeed, in one of his last public statements he attacked the way the British public had received Garibaldi in 1864. Wiseman was too good a papalist to allow any suitable occasion to pass by without defending his patrons in Rome.

Inevitably the whole question of the establishment of the hierarchy was bound to be discussed in one or more numbers of the *Dublin Review.* Following the uproar when he was named Cardinal Archbishop, he wrote a long piece in December 1850. As was customary, he used works by various authors such as John Henry Newman and George Errington as well as a number of anonymous writers who had produced pamphlets on the question. Surprizingly, he also included his own *Appeal.* Normally, of course, the writer of an article used the works of other people but Wiseman was a law unto himself. Indeed, in this instance he was not really reviewing anything or anybody, although he did use ideas and statements from other people, but rather he was simply restating for a Roman Catholic audience his own position and that of Rome. This was really a form of allocation for, aside from his *Appeal,* he made no real effort to win public sympathy. Wiseman in this case was writing for his own people. However, not all Roman Catholics had approved of Rome's decision; they thought the whole business very ill-advised, and treated it as evidence of the increased 'Romanization' of their Church by Wiseman and his supporters in contrast to the earlier and simpler days. To rebut such critics, a second article on the same subject appeared in the following March. In both, Wiseman explained the whole question of the legality of Rome's action and lessened much of the criticism by showing what had been done in Canada and Ireland. In addition, he indicated that in both instances the action taken by Rome had the support and approbation of the governments in those places. A third and final article appeared in September 1851, but by this time public interest in the subject was exhausted, and the Great Exhibition had captured the popular attention. 'No Popery' was no longer an issue.

However, the fact that he still felt it necessary to write several long pieces — the first twenty-seven pages and the second thirty-one — demonstrated that he felt he must justify his actions on his own home front and is an indication also of how significant he felt opposition sentiment to be even in his own communion. With the public at large his case had been won by his *Appeal* in December 1850, and this despite the passage of the Ecclesiastical Titles Act.

The number of articles written by him had declined steadily in the years following the establishment of the hierarchy. In the mid-1850's there was a renewed spate of activity, but thereafter fewer and fewer of his articles were published. Indeed, one can see that his other duties now supervened and that he did not have the time for literary pursuits. At the best of times he could never give his full time to such activities and it is quite astounding that he wrote as much as he did. In many ways Wiseman was better as an editor and author for he was generally incapable as an administrator of the Church. Indeed, he might have been happier if he had confined himself to the world of literature and scholarship, for he enjoyed writing and he had his century's flair and confidence to tackle almost any subject. Over the years Wiseman wrote something in the order of seventy articles in the *Dublin Review*. For a cleric with other responsibilities this is quite astounding, and if one recollects that Wiseman was a cardinal and an archbishop for fifteen years, it is amazing. Moreover, it should be remembered that these articles in the *Dublin Review* were but a small part of his literary output.

Certainly the *Dublin Review* never had the wide influence of the *Quarterly Review*, for example, but for literate Roman Catholic households it was a significant organ. Moreover, if anyone wished to know Roman Catholic sentiment on public affairs, the *Review* was a good indicator, and with the increased number of Roman Catholics in substantial positions in society, especially following the Oxford Movement, this body of opinion could not be neglected.

Wiseman was a child of his own century and he believed in the importance of the written word, recognizing its influence in his day. Perhaps the best summation of his own position with respect to the *Review* appears in the final article which he himself contributed. It was his own valedictory for it was published in November 1862; the new series and basically a very changed review appeared the following year. Wiseman summed up what he had done:

> From the first number to this, every article has been written, or revised, under the sense of the most solemn responsibility to the church, and to her Lord. If we have been reproached, it

has been rather for severity in exclusion, than for laxity in admission. Many an article has been ejected rather than rejected, even after being in type, because it was found not to accord with the high and strict principles from which its editorship was never swerved, and which it has never abated. To him who has conducted it for so many years, a higher praise could scarcely be given; and by no one, we are sure, has it ever been better deserved. That occasionally an article, or a passage may have crept in, which did not perfectly come up to the highest standard of ecclesiastical judgment, is not only possible but probable. Absence, hurry, pressing occupation, ill-health, or even inadvertence and justifiable confidence will be sufficient to account for an occasional deviation from role, should anyone think he detects it. If so, we are certain he will find its corrective or its rectification in some other place.

For from first to last, as we have said, this Review has been guided by principles fixed and unalterable; and those who have conducted it, have done so with the feeling that they must render an account of all that they admitted. However, long may be its duration, and under whatever auspices, we are sure that the same deep, earnest, and religious sense will pervade its pages, and animate its conductors, that their occupation is a sacred one, a deputation to posterity that our children's children maw know how we adhered to the *true faith* of their fathers, how we bore with patience and *gentleness* the persecutions of our enemies, and how we never swerved from *justice* to friend or foe. Our motto may well be: PROPTER VERITATEM, ET MANSUETUDINEM ET JUSTITIAM.' [5]

NOTES

Notes to Chapter 1

1　There are three full-length biographical studies of Nicholas Wiseman. The first, by Wilfrid Ward, *The Life and Times of Cardinal Wiseman* in two volumes was published in 1897. It is highly idiosyncratic, very biassed and distinctly hagiographic but, like Lockhart's biography of Sir Walter Scott, it is essential that it be consulted, for it captures, more specifically, the spirit of its subject than do the later works. The second, by Denis Gwynn entitled *Cardinal Wiseman*, appeared half a century later — is this perhaps not indicative of the way Wiseman was possibly regarded by his co-religionists as well as by historians? — and is based largely upon printed materials. It is an orderly and straightforward account by a professional historian presenting the narrative of Wiseman's life. Generally it is not overly critical. The third, and most recent volume on the subject, is by Brian Fothergill and is simply called *Nicholas Wiseman*, and was published in 1963. It, too, is largely based on the printed materials but is more lively than Gwynn's book. Fothergill is sympathetic to Wiseman — it is difficult not to be despite his obvious failngs — and for the general reader t is the most complete account to date. One day Wiseman will be the subject of a proper and full-scale biographical study based upon his papers and other similar sources but until that time these biographies will have to serve.

2　The general outline of Wiseman's life is taken from the three previously mentioned biographical studies as well as the usual obituary notices that appeared in the public press after his death.

3　As quoted in Ward, Vol. I, p. 15.

4　Dr. Robert Gradwell, quoted in Ward, Vol. I, p. 26.

5　Nicholas Wiseman, quoted in Ward, Vol. I, p. 29.

6　Nicholas Wiseman, quoted in Ward, Vol. I, pp. 71–72.

7　Nicholas Wiseman, quoted in Ward, Vol. I, p. 123.

8　Nicholas Wiseman, quoted in Fothergill, p. 71.

9　Nicholas Wiseman to Monckton Milnes, September 1835 as quoted in Ward, Vol. I, p. 215.

10　*Loc. cit.*

11　Nicholas Wiseman, *Lectures*, etc. (Booker, London, 1830), p. 20.

12　W. E. Gladstone, quoted in Ward, Vol. I, p. 248.

13　Nicholas Wiseman, quoted in Ward, Vol. I, p. 245.

14　Nicholas Wiseman, 'Resolutions Made at the Exercises of November 1837', quoted in Ward, Vol. I, p. 263.

15　Ronald Chapman, *Father Faber*, p. 249.

16　Nicholas Wiseman to Father Ignatius Spencer, quoted in Ward, Vol. I, p. 305.

17　Nicholas Wiseman to Xaviera Wiseman, 11 October, 1839, quoted in Ward, Vol. I, p. 311.

18　Nicholas Wiseman to Countess Gabrielli, 27 April, 1839, quoted in Fothergill, p. 60.

19　Nicholas Wiseman to Bagshawe, 16 November, 1839, quoted in Ward, Vol. I, p. 335.

20　Nicholas Wiseman to Countess Gabrielli, 27 April, 1839, quoted in Fothergill, pp. 79–80.

21　Nicholas Wiseman, 1857, quoted in Ward, Vol. I, p. 340.

22 Lord Acton, quoted in Ward, Vol. I, p. 349.
23 Nicholas Wiseman to Ambrose Phillips de Lisle, April, 1841, quoted in Fothergill, p. 104.
24 Quoted in Ward, Vol. I, p. 379.
25 Nicholas Wiseman to Rev. Dr. Russell, 1844, quoted in Ward, Vol. I, p. 421.
26 Nicholas Wiseman to Rev. J. H. Newsham, 26 November, 1848, quoted in Ward, Vol. I, p. 507.
27 *Loc cit.*
28 From the middle of October 1850 for the next few weeks 'Papal Aggression' was kept before the public in a series of articles in *The Times.*
29 Nicholas Wiseman, quoted in Ward, Vol. I, p. 532.
30 John Henry Newman to Sir George Bowyer, quoted in Ward, Vol. I, p. 534.
31 Nicholas Wiseman to Lord John Russell, 3 November, 1850, quoted in Ward, Vol. I, p. 535.
32 For Queen Victoria on the subject see *The Letters of Queen Victoria . . . 1837–1867,* (John Murray, London, 1907), Vol. II, pp. 325–326, pp. 331–332, pp. 334–335, pp. 336–337.
33 Fothergill, p. 169.
34 Quoted in Ward, Vol. I, p. 554.
35 Duke of Norfolk to Lord Beaumont, 28 November, 1850, quoted in Ward, Vol. II, p. 15.
36 Archbishop George Errington to Monsignor George Talbot, 23 August, 1855, quoted in Ward, Vol. II, p. 262.
37 Monsignor George Talbot to Archbishop George Errington, 17 April, 1859, quoted in Ward, Vol. II, p. 333.
38 Nicholas Wiseman on 5 February, 1865, quoted in Ward, Vol. II, p. 515.
39 This summation of Nicholas Wiseman did not appear in a Roman Catholic publication but in *The Patriot* which was one of the leading journals of the non-conformist conscience. Hence, it is all the more significant to read it in this publication which was often very critical of Wiseman. Quoted in Ward, Vol. II, p. 521.

Notes to Chapter 2

1 Nicholas Wiseman, 'Preface', *Essays on Various Subjects* (Charles Dolman, London 1853), Vol. II, p. viii. Hereafter referred to as Wiseman, *Essays.*
2 *Loc. cit.*
3 Wiseman, 'Preface', *Essays,* Vol. II, p. x.
4 Lord David Cecil, *Lord M. or The Later Life of Lord Melbourne,* (Constable, London 1954), p. 142.
5 Wiseman, 'The Hampden Controversy', *Essays,* Vol. II, pp. 5–6.
6 Wiseman, 'The Hampden Controversy', *Essays,* Vol. II, p. 14.
7 Wiseman, 'The Hampden Controversy', *Essays,* Vol. II, p. 25.
8 Wiseman, 'The Hampden Controversy', *Essays,* Vol. II, p. 26.
9 Wiseman, 'Tracts for the Times', *Essays,* Vol. II, p. 39.
10 Wiseman, 'Tracts for the Times', *Essays,* Vol. II, p. 47.
11 Wiseman, 'Tracts for the Times', *Essays,* Vol. II, p. 59.
12 Wiseman, 'Tracts for the Times', *Essays,* Vol. II, p. 61.

13 Wiseman, 'Anglican Claims', *Essays*, Vol. II, p. 166.
14 Wiseman, 'Anglican Claims', *Essays*, Vol. II, p. 167.
15 Canon of the Council of Nicea, 325 A.D. quoted in Wiseman, 'Anglican Claims', *Essays*, Vol. II, p. 171.
16 Wiseman, 'Anglican Claims', *Essays*, Vol. II, p. 175.
17 Wiseman, 'Anglican Claims', *Essays*, Vol. II, pp. 175–180 *passim*.
18 Wiseman, 'Anglican Claims', *Essays*, Vol. II, p. 197.
19 Wiseman, 'Anglican Claims', *Essays*, Vol. II, p. 195.
20 St. Augustine, quoted in footnote in Wiseman, 'The Catholic and Anglican Churches', *Essays*, Vol. II, p. 206.
21 Wiseman, 'The Catholic and Anglican Churches', *Essays*, Vol. II, p. 216.
22 St. Augustine, quoted in Wiseman, 'The Catholic and Anglican Churches', *Essays*, Vol. II, p. 227.
23 Wiseman, 'The Catholic and Anglican Churches', *Essays*, Vol. II, p. 250.
24 Wiseman, 'The Catholic and Anglican Churches', *Essays*, Vol. II, p. 267.
25 St. Cyprian, quoted in Wiseman, 'The Anglican System', *Essays*, Vol. II, p. 312.
26 Wiseman, 'The Anglican System', *Essays*, Vol. II, p. 317.
27 Wiseman, 'The Anglican System', *Essays*, Vol. II, p. 328.
28 Wiseman, 'Unreality of Anglican Belief', *Essays*, Vol. II, pp. 418–419.
29 John Keble, *Sermons Academical and Otherwise*, p. 21, quoted in Wiseman, 'Position of High Church Theory', *Essays*, Vol. II, p. 445.
30 Wiseman, 'The Anglican System', *Essays*, Vol. II, p. 327.
31 Wiseman, 'Froude's Remains', *Essays*, Vol. II, p. 102.
32 Herbert Vaughan, *Meditations on the Sacred Passion of Our Lord* (Burns and Oates, London, 1898), p. ix.

Notes to Chapter 3

1 Nicholas Wiseman, *On the Perception of Natural Beauty by the Ancients and Moderns* (London, 1856), p. 2, hereafter referred to as *Perception*.
2 Wiseman, *Perception*, p. 3.
3 Wiseman, *Perception*, p. 10.
4 Wiseman, *Perception*, p. 12.
5 Wiseman, *Perception*, p. 14.
6 Wiseman, *Perception*, p. 21.
7 *Loc. cit.*
8 Wiseman, *Perception*, p. 23.
9 Wiseman, *Perception*, p. 26.
10 Wiseman, *Perception*, p. 34.
11 *Loc. cit.*
12 Wiseman, *Perception*, p. 34.
13 Nicholas Wiseman, 'Philosophy of Art', *Dublin Review*, No. 1, 1836, p. 438. Hereafter referred to as 'Philosophy of Art'.
14 Wiseman, 'Philosophy of Art', p. 439.
15 *Loc. cit.*
16 Wiseman, 'Philosophy of Art', p. 442.
17 Wiseman, 'Philosophy of Art', p. 446.
18 *Loc. cit.*
19 Wiseman, 'Philosophy of Art', p. 447.

Wiseman, 'Philosophy of Art', p. 450.

21 Wiseman, 'Philosophy of Art', p. 456.

22 Wiseman, *Recollections of the Last Four Popes*, p. 166, hereafter referred to as *Recollections*.

23 *Loc. cit.*

24 Wiseman, *Recollections*, p. 167.

25 Wiseman, 'Christian Art', *Essays*, Vol. III, pp. 258-359.

26 Wiseman, 'Christian Art', *Essays*, Vol. III, p. 359.

27 *Loc. cit.*

28 Wiseman, 'Christian Art', *Essays*, Vol. III, p. 361.

29 *Loc. cit.*

30 Wiseman, 'Christian Art', *Essays*, Vol. III, p. 361.

31 Wiseman, 'Christian Art', *Essays*, Vol. III, p. 363.

32 Wiseman, 'Christian Art', *Essays*, Vol. III, p. 364.

33 Wiseman, 'Christian Art', *Essays*, Vol. III, p. 365.

34 Wiseman, 'Christian Art', *Essays*, Vol. III, pp. 369-370.

35 Wiseman, 'Christian Art', *Essays*, Vol. III, p. 375.

36 *Loc. cit.*

37 Wiseman, 'Christian Art', *Essays*, Vol. III, p. 384.

38 Wiseman, 'Christian Art', *Essays*, Vol. III, p. 385.

39 Wiseman, 'Christian Art', *Essays*, Vol. III, p. 387.

40 Wiseman, 'Spanish and English National Art', *Essays*, Vol. III, p. 397, hereafter referred to as 'National Art', *Essays*, etc.

41 *Loc. cit.*

42 Wiseman, 'National Art', *Essays*, Vol. III, p. 399.

43 Wiseman, 'National Art', *Essays*, Vol. III, p. 400.

44 In his article entitled 'Christian Art', *Essays*, Vol. III, p. 381, Wiseman states categorically 'Not one Englishman in ten thousand has an opportunity of seeing a truly religious painting; not one in ten times that number, of seeing so many and such as can form his taste, and enable him to appreciate this highest form of art.'

45 Wiseman, 'National Art', *Essays*, Vol. III, p. 416.

46 c.f. the long quotation from Lord Lindsay's *Sketches of Christian Art*, in Wiseman 'Christian Art', *Essays*, Vol. III, pp. 391-392 and Wiseman's comments on it.

47 Wiseman, 'National Art', *Essays*, Vol. III, p. 417.

48 *Loc. cit.*

49 Wiseman, 'National Art', *Essays*, Vol. III, p. 418.

50 *Loc. cit.*

51 Wiseman, 'National Art', *Essays*, Vol. III, p. 419.

52 Wiseman, 'National Art', *Essays*, Vol. III, p. 431.

53 Wiseman, 'National Art', *Essays*, Vol. III, p. 433.

54 Wiseman, 'Philosophy of Art', *Dublin Review*, No. 1, 1836, p. 438.

55 Wiseman, 'Philosophy of Art', p. 439.

56 *Loc. cit.*

57 Wiseman, 'Philosophy of Art', p. 459.

58 For Wiseman's views on ecclesiastical architecture generally see his 'Ecclesiastical Architecture', *Dublin Review*, No. 6, 1837, and also his article 'Christian Art', *Essays*, Vol. III.

59 As quoted in B. Fothergill, *Nicholas Wiseman*, p. 46.

60 Wiseman, 'National Art', *Essays*, Vol. III, p. 424.

61 Wiseman, 'Christian Art', *Essays*, Vol. III, p. 371.

62 Wiseman, 'Christian Art', *Essays*, Vol. III, p. 359.

Notes to Chapter 4

1 A short account of some of the publishing history of *Fabiola* may serve to illustrate its rather special story. For a literary work that must be considered minor, it has had far more editions than would seem warranted. The first edition appeared in London in 1855 as part of The Catholic Popular Library series under their imprint and cost three shillings and sixpence. A second edition was published in the same year by Burns and Oates. It continued to be reprinted by the latter firm: further editions appeared in 1870, 1896, 1904, 1906 and then again in 1962. It had equal success in the United States; D. & J. Sadlier published an edition in 1855, and another in 1874, a rival firm, Benzinger Brothers, republished it in 1886 and 1896. A school edition was printed by Longmans of New York in 1932, another and revised edition was put out by Kennedy publishers in 1951; The Daughters of St. Paul Press in Derby, N.Y. reprinted a new edition in 1956 and the Newman Press in Westminster, Maryland, brought out yet another edition in 1972. There are at least two French versions, one in 1891 and another published by Nelsons of Edinburgh and Paris in 1935. A Russian edition was published in Moscow in 1866 and again in 1886, an Hungarian edition appeared in Budapest in 1856, a Romansch edition in 1897, two Spanish versions, the first in Bogota, Columbia, in 1865 and a second in Madrid in 1956, and an edition in Irish was put out in Dublin in 1939. Even Esperanto was used as a language for one edition which was printed in Geneva in 1911. *Fabiola* was rewritten as a play by F. Oakley under the title *The Youthful Martyrs of Rome* in 1856 while a French version was prepared by M. Soullier as a drama in three acts 'pour demoiselles'. A film was made of the story by an Italian company in 1949. From this rather brief and incomplete bibliographic note it is evident that *Fabiola* succeeded far beyond the modest aims of its author.

A somewhat cursory perusal of the well-known bibliographic aids show that Newman, although an infinitely better known writer, did not have quite as much success. Editions of *Callista* appeared in England in 1856, 1876, 1880, 1885, 1890, 1901, 1904 and 1906, but aside from being included in Newman's Collected Works, completed in 1921, the book appears to have gone out of print in Britain. There were a couple of editions in the U.S.A. in the nineteenth century and one at the beginning of this century. The book was also published in Prague in 1887 and in France in 1890. A dramatic version entitled *The Convent Martyr*, appeared in 1857.

2 From *A Few Flowers from the Roman Campagna*, (London, John Philip), 1861.

Notes to Chapter 5

1 Reprinted as 'Pope Boniface VIII', *Essays on Various Subjects*, Vol. III, pp. 161-222, hereafter referred to as Wiseman, Pope Boniface VIII, *Essays*, etc.
2 Nicholas Wiseman, Pope Boniface VIII, *Essays*, Vol. III, p. 162.
3 Nicholas Wiseman, *Four Advent Lectures on Concordats*, 1855, No. 1, p. 3.
4 Nicholas Wiseman, *Four Advent Lectures etc.*, No. 1, p. 4.

5   Nicholas Wiseman, *Four Advent Lectures etc.*, No. 3, p. 14.
6   Nicholas Wiseman, *Four Advent Lectures etc.*, No. 3, p. 18.
7   Nicholas Wiseman, *Four Advent Lectures etc.*, No. 3, p. 9.
8   Nicholas Wiseman uses historical evidence in a similar fashion in his 'St. Elizabeth of Hungary', *Dublin Review*, October 1837, 'Brief Account of the Council Held at Constantinople, A.D. 1166', from the *Catholic Magazine* and 'Authority of the Holy See in South America', *Dublin Review*, July 1838.
9   Nicholas Wiseman, *Recollections of the Last Four Popes and of Rome in Their Times*, 1858, p. v, hereafter referred to as *Recollections etc.*
10 Nicholas Wiseman, *Recollections, etc.*, p. vi.
11 Nicholas Wiseman, *Recollections, etc.*, p. 30.
12 Nicholas Wiseman, *Recollections, etc.*, p. 227.
13 Nicholas Wiseman, *Recollections, etc.*, p. 372.
14 Nicholas Wiseman, *Recollections, etc.*, p. 506.
15 Nicholas Wiseman, *Recollections, etc.*, p. 223, note 1.
16 Nicholas Wiseman, *Recollections, etc.*, p. 332.
17 Nicholas Wiseman, *Recollections, etc.*, p. 340.
18 Nicholas Wiseman, *Recollections, etc.*, pp. 164-165.
19 Nicholas Wiseman, *Recollections, etc.*, p. 165.
20 Nicholas Wiseman, *Recollections, etc.*, p. 166.
21 Nicholas Wiseman, *Recollections, etc.*, p. 196.
22 Nicholas Wiseman, *Recollections, etc.*, p. 421.
23 Nicholas Wiseman, *Recollections, etc.*, p. 428.
24 Nicholas Wiseman, *Recollections, etc.*, pp. 428-429.
25 Nicholas Wiseman, *Recollections, etc.*, p. 429.
26 Nicholas Wiseman, *Recollections, etc.*, pp. 513-514.
27 Nicholas Wiseman, *Lectures on Science and Revealed Religion*, No. 7, pp. 255-256, hereafter referred to as *Lectures on Science, etc.*
28 Nicholas Wiseman, *Lectures on Science, etc.*, No. 6, p. 254.

Notes to Chapter 6

1   Wilfrid Ward, *Life and Times of Cardinal Wiseman*, Vol. I, p. 249.
2   Wilfrid Ward, *Cardinal Wiseman*, Vol. I, p. 252.
3   *Loc. cit.*
4   Professor Denis Gwyn sums up Wiseman's rôle as editor of the *Dublin Review*: 'It gave him an invaluable link with the friends he had made in England, and it brought him in contact with a number of distinguished Irish writers. . . . Among the educated Catholics of London he had established a definite position of intellectual leadership.' Denis Gwyn, *Cardinal Wiseman*, p. 43.
5   Nicholas Wiseman, 'On Responsibility', *Dublin Review*, November 1862, pp. 183-184.

INDEX

141